Y0-ACG-399

M in the Canadian Rockies IXED CLIMBS

Sean Isaac

Disclaimer

There are inherent risks in mixed climbing. While the author has done his best to provide accurate information and to point out potential hazards, conditions may change owing to weather and other factors. It is up to the users of this guide to learn the necessary skills for safe mixed climbing and to exercise caution in potentially hazardous areas. Please read the "Avalanches" and "Other Hazards" sections in the introduction to this book.

Climbers using this book do so entirely at their own risk and the author and publishers disclaim any liability for injury or other damage that may be sustained by anyone using the access and/or climbing routes described.

Front cover: Kim Csizmazia swinging onto Ain't Nobody Here But Us Chickens. *Photo Will Gadd.*
Back cover: Raphael Slawinski slays the Mixed Monster. *Photo Eamonn Walsh.*

We acknowledge the financial support of the Government of Canada through the
Book Publishing Industry Development Program (BPIDP) for our publishing activities.

All rights reserved. No part of this work may be
reproduced or transmitted in any form or by any
means, electronic or mechanical, including
photocopying and recording, or by any information
storage or retrieval system, except as may be
expressly permitted in writing from the publisher.

Copyright © 2000 Sean Isaac

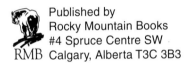 Published by
Rocky Mountain Books
#4 Spruce Centre SW
RMB Calgary, Alberta T3C 3B3

Printed and bound in Canada by
Houghton Boston, Saskatoon

ISBN 0-921102-81-X

Canadian Cataloguing in Publication Data

Isaac, Sean, 1972-
 Mixed climbs in the Canadian Rockies

 Includes index.
 ISBN 0-921102-81-X

 1. Rock climbing--Rocky Mountains, Canadian (B.C. and Alta.)--Guidebooks.*
2. Snow and ice climbing--Rocky Mountains, Canadian (B.C. and Alta.)--Guidebooks.*
I. Title.
GV199.44.C22R62787 2000   796.52'23'09711   C00-911081-X

CONTENTS

Climbing Areas

Information

ACKNOWLEDGMENTS

Writing a guidebook is only accomplished with the assistance of many people contributing information. By no means have I done or will I ever do all of the routes in this guide, so other climbers' beta is key. Essentially, I have just compiled the details and presented them in an orderly fashion.

Special thanks is necessary for a few individuals who have gone out of their way to aid this project: Will Gadd for his motivating foreword; Raphael Slawinski for answering all of my pestering emails (he has done most of the routes in this guide); Joe Josephson for his guidebook *Waterfall Ice Climbs in the Canadian Rockies*, which was a huge help in compiling information; Geoff Powter for his topo making tips; and Dave Thomson for his mentoring, vision and great routes.

Thanks also go to the following for their route descriptions:
Mike Adolf, Bill Belcourt, Barry Blanchard, Joe Buszowski, Dave Campbell, Sean Elliot, Jeff Everett, Ben Firth, Tyler Freed, Will Gadd, Jim Gudjonson, Keith Haberl, Bruce Hendricks, Doug Heinrich, Steve House, Joe Josephson, David Marra, Allan Massin, Joe McKay, Rob Owens, Jeff Perron, Raphael Slawinski, Grant Statham, Margot Talbot, Dave Thomson, Geoff Trump, Jyoti Venne, Eamonn Walsh, Brian Webster, Ken Wylie.

Also to all the folks who provided a great selection of photos for us to choose from: Serge Angelucci, Glen Boles, Dave Campbell, Roger Chayer, Darcy Chilton, Matt Collins, Brian Cox, David Dornian, Jeff Everett, Will Gadd, Jim Gudjonson, Keith Haberl, Bruce Hendricks, Jeff Honig, Steve House, Shawn and Shelly Huisman, Joe Josephson, Troy Kirwan, Rob Owens, Tim Pochay, Black and White Productions, Glen Reisenhofer, Raphael Slawinski, Grant Statham, Dave Thomson, Geoff Trump, Brad Wrobleski.

When the temperatures start to dip below freezing at night, I have a hard time sleeping, and work is simply out of the question. I know icicles are forming drip by drip in the shelter of dark limestone caves, ephemeral smears come and go, old photos are scanned for new prospects and the taste of ice is everywhere. Binoculars are produced, long walks to nonexistent climbs are undertaken, tools are filed to surgical specifications, and every degree below zero is met with increasing glee. In the fall of '99 we all existed in a web where each new route and rumour of fresh ice vibrated via phone lines, email and gossip in the grocery store check-out line. The efforts of Raphael Slawinski, Dave Mara, Sean Isaac, Rob Owens, Ben Firth, Dave Thomson, Eamonn Walsh, Icebacks from the States and a host of tracks into hidden projects by unknown climbers ("Can't be Raph, he wears Scarpas. Who the hell scooped us!?"), meant that no icicle was safe. If you think I'm exaggerating then you don't know the half of it. Some weekdays last winter saw not one, but three or four new routes done in a day, often of super high quality. I grew up climbing in the Canadian Rockies, but I can't think of a time in the last 20 years where so much was happening.

All this is occurring despite the fact Joe Josephson, author of the excellent ice guide, had prophesied that all the good lines in the Rockies were done (sorry Jo Jo, ya said it). If we were looking for pure ice lines, he was right. As much as I admire the earlier generations of ice climbers in the Rockies, I had also always felt annoyed that they plucked so many of the jewels, selfish bastards. But mixed climbing opened up a fresh freezer, laden with frozen delicacies that were more than simply ice from bottom to top, but ornamental hanging daggers and candy-bar thick ice smears streaking black faces on wild walls. Dave Thomson, Sean Isaac, Kefira Allen, Eric Dumerac and many others were already in full swing when I arrived in '98; it was their photos and stories that showed me where I wanted to live. Yet as deep as they were digging, plums still hung everywhere, just asking for tools and a creative mind. Today, unlike 10 years ago when I too thought everything was done, I feel lucky to live in a place with so many great mixed lines to climb, and so many more yet to do. I have climbed mixed routes all over the world, but the Rockies are simply bigger and badder with more to do than any range I've ever seen.

The routes in this book are a great beginning, but only a beginning. Future volumes will be thicker, wilder, woollier! One can't drive down the Icefields Parkway in winter without several near-ditch experiences and a case of whiplash from eyeballing the possibilities; before this book you might even have climbed a "new" route, only to discover that the likes of Allan Massin or Jeff Everett did it five years ago but forgot to mention it to anyone. *Mixed Climbs in the Canadian Rockies* will help climbers find these new classics (and how can *Rocket Man*, the *Big Drip*, *Nightmare on Wolf Street* and so many other good routes become anything but classics?), as well as the future ones. From the short M-hard afternoon desperate climbs of Haffner Creek to pre-dawn starts and battery-powered finishes on multi-pitch monsters, the mixed Rockies await. Just file your picks and never, ever hit the big icicles too hard!

Will Gadd, Canmore 2000

INTRODUCTION

Mixed climbing is climbing on both ice and rock, either in quick succession or actually at the same time.
Yvon Chouinard, "Climbing Ice" (1978).

The Canadian Rockies are a mixed climbers mecca. With so much terrain and such a long season, it is no wonder Rockies' routes and Rockies' climbers are at the cutting edge of the modern mixed game. In the past five years, mixed climbing has seen an explosion in popularity. With many more participants and an ever increasing number of new routes, a guidebook covering solely mixed climbs was in order.

A year ago I decided it was time to fill the gap and compile the scattered route information into a single volume. Magazine articles, Internet sites and word-of-mouth were the only sources of information on the rapidly growing number of mixed lines. What began as a low key, self-published, home-generated guide has evolved into the book you hold now.

Twenty years ago, Albi Sole saw the demand for the world's first ice climbing guidebook, *Waterfall Ice Climbs in the Canadian Rockies*. Once again, Canadian Rockies' winter climbers are leading the way with the world's first mixed-waterfall ice guidebook, *Mixed Climbs in the Canadian Rockies*. It covers 158 mixed routes ranging from the time-honored classics of Joe Josephson's *Waterfall Ice, 3rd Edition* to the modern sport-style testpieces of the new millennium.

Of course, there are bound to be a few mistakes and as the author I expect to be endlessly slagged for every little flaw. I have not climbed every mixed route and don't anticipate doing so. I must, therefore, rely heavily on secondhand beta. I hope the details described within are accurate and you enjoy reading and using this guidebook.

The book is not only supposed to be an information resource, I would also like to think of it as a motivational piece. It is packed with exciting photographs that will surely get your adrenaline surging. Both local and international climbers alike should benefit from its pages.

HISTORY

Early mountaineers used mixed climbing as a means to an end. They would often be forced to scratch up snowy rock or thin ice on alpine routes to get to easier ground in order to gain a summit. Like rock climbing, mixed climbing eventually evolved into a sport unto its own pursued for its movement and athletics. The past 10 years especially have seen increased interest and growth in the sport. The mixed game has been elevated to vogue status and is also excellent training for big routes in the high mountains.

In the early 1980s, ice climbers were already getting bored with the tediousness of vertical ice and craved something more dynamic in winter climbing. The logical progression was to seek thinner and thinner ice routes until sections of rock were used to link these discontinuous smears.

This was already occurring on the big north face routes like *Andromeda*

Strain, Grand Central Couloir and *Humble Horse*, but it wasn't until the late 1980s that people started practising it on smaller cliffs.

Mixed climbing really caught on in 1991 with the now classic *Mixed Master* receiving the most attention. Located only 10 minutes from the highway, right beside the very popular Weeping Wall, veteran ice climbers could not believe they never had seen this gem. It wasn't because the route wasn't there before; it was because they simply weren't looking for that sort of thing. Almost instantly, eyes opened and winter climbers were discovering the potential of putting ice tools and crampons to rock. The spring of 1991 saw another major breakthrough with Jeff Everett's and Glen Reisenhofer's futuristic *Suffer Machine* on the Stanley Headwall. This massive waterfall had never formed completely, always ending as an unformed icicle hanging over a cave. That year it came tantalizingly close to the ground so the duo humped an extension ladder up the two hour approach with the intention of using it to gain the ice. Of course, the ladder was too short so they returned armed with a full aid rack and bolt kit and proceeded to climb the rock up the steep wall to the ice.

The next couple of years, local activists were busy searching for unformed ice. Armed with the mottos "less is more" and "it doesn't have to be formed to be formed," Barry Blanchard, Joe Josephson, Tim Pochay, Bruce Hendricks, Joe Buszowski, Grant Statham, Peter Arbic, Karl Nagy and others changed their views. They now regarded WI5 bashing as stale and thin ice and rock as fresh. Numerous traditional classics were discovered: *Shampoo Planet, Red Man Soars, French Reality, Auto de Feu*, and the much publi-

cized *Sea of Vapors* on Mount Rundle. The first ascent of *Sea of Vapors* by Josephson and Hendricks was a super bold effort requiring challenging thin ice and mixed climbing way above bad gear. Since then, it has always formed fatter taking away much of its sting.

It was primarily American climbers who pushed standards on Mount Rundle in the mid-'90s with the creation of two sick lines: *Troubled Dreams* by Hendricks and Scott Backes, which was later freed in a bold tour de force by Alex Lowe; and *Two Piece Yanks* by Steve House and Stan Price.

Sport-style mixed climbing with bolt protection took awhile longer to catch on here than in the United States, but when it did, locals fully realized the potential that our mountains held. Anthony Nielson made the breakthrough in 1997 with the Rockies' first bolted mixed route. His *Mental Jewelry* in Grotto Canyon instantly saw huge traffic. Traditional climbing was also rapidly advancing with Raphael Slawinski's and Matt Collins' first free ascent and second ascent overall of T*he Day After les Vacances de Monsieur Hulot* on the Stanley Headwall. This testpiece was originally climbed with extensive aid, which Slawinski and Collins eliminated on-sight at M7 R. Many of the routes from the early '90s used aid, but as dry tooling skills improved, the aid on old mixed disappeared and new routes were being put up free.

It was Dave Thomson, though, who embraced the new "sport" philosophy and charged full steam ahead with his drill leading the way. His vision and commitment forged over 30 superb mixed routes in only four seasons, establishing him as the "Father of Modern Rockies Mixed Climbing."

The winter of 1997/1998 saw an unprecedented amount of new multi-pitch mixed routes of staggering difficulty. Dave Thomson and Sean Isaac made close to 30 trips to the Stanley Headwall that season, allowing them to double the amount of routes. Most of the routes sported bolt protection for the extremely technical rock sections; however, these were by no means sport routes. The ice was still your regular old, hard-to-protect WI6 shake-fest. Big falls were still available despite the bolts as Slawinski demonstrated while attempting the second ascent of *Teddy Bear's Picnic*. He managed to on-sight the overhanging M8 rock but snapped the hanging curtain near the end of the pitch sending him for a 30 m whipper that he miraculously walked away from.

Other notable multi-pitch routes to be climbed that year included *Mixed Monster, Stairway to Heaven, Jacob's Ladder* and *The Unicorn*, all by various combinations of Thomson, Isaac, Kafira Allen and Eric Dumerac.

Meanwhile, Field in Yoho National Park was coughing up a number of fun single-pitch routes, most of which were of the traditional genre. Over 20 new lines went in by a variety of players including Jim Gudjonson, Allan Massin and Steve Pratt.

Things continued much along the same track the next year with more cutting edge monstrosities created. *The Real Big Drip, Nightmare on Wolf Street* and *Rocket Man* illustrated that the Canadian Rockies held huge potential for long, hard mixed routes. These were opened by the same players as the previous year with the addition of Slawinski getting in on the new route scene. *Rocket Man* embodies everything that modern mixed climbing represents with its long hazardous approach, committing position, 350 m of technical mixed climbing, both bolted and traditional protection and, to polish off the difficulties, an unprotected M6+ as the final pitch.

The 1999/2000 season took a different turn. As the most obvious big prizes had been plucked, climbers shifted their attention toward pushing the standards on single-pitch sport-style routes. New "sport areas" like Haffner Creek and Waterfowl Gullies were being developed at a rapid pace. Simultaneously, the overall technical level of the community soared with M8s being on-sighted regularly and a handful of M9s established. The first M9 in Canada was Will Gadd's *Power to Burn* at Waterfowl Gullies. Even these top end routes were seeing constant traffic with people hopping on them and working their relatively safe moves. The closing of the season saw the opening of two of the technically hardest mixed pitches in North America. Sean Isaac made the first ascent of the horizontal *Caveman*, checking in at M9+. The other new testpiece was Ben Firth's and Raphael Slawinski's *Animal Farm* at the Gulag on Mount Rundle. Tentatively rated at M9+, this could actually be North America's first M10.

Hard but not that hard, these routes are only the beginning. The next few years will definitely see more M10s and M11s being sent as well as on-sights of increasingly harder routes. However, the future of Canadian Rockies' mixed climbing is not 30 m cragging routes. The future is once again changing our perception of what is possible: multi-pitch M10s, traditional M9s, serious run-out M8s. The Canadian Rockies has unlimited potential for those with the vision.

HOW TO USE THIS GUIDE

This guide uses a combination of maps, written descriptions, topos and photos to help explain the location and nature of a specific mixed route.

Areas are presented from south to north beginning with Waterton National Park and finishing with the Jasper area.

Every route has a written description ranging from one line to a full page. These include access and approach information, a general route description or pitch by pitch account and descent beta. I have also made it a point to mention whether a route or its approach is threatened by avalanche danger. All descriptions using right and left as directions are looking up at the climb i.e., climbers right or climbers left.

Some routes have topos to better illustrate them. These topos are not to scale and are to be used in conjunction with the description to get an idea of the general layout of a route. Bolt counts on the topos (i.e., number of little x's) should be correct but always carry an extra quick draw or two just in case. The position of the bolts on the topos are not exact. Remember that removable fixed protection like pitons, Specters and stoppers can change so be prepared to replace them.

The back of the book contains a list of all the routes with their grade and first ascent information including names of the first ascensionists and the month and year they were climbed. The climbers' names are in alphabetical order (according to the last name) regardless who lead the route or the crux. Multi-pitch mixed climbing is a team effort. Often times only one name will be listed for single-pitch sport style routes. This usu-ally means the first ascensionist bolted the route by himself and then found a belayer for the redpoint. It doesn't mean the route was soloed. In the occurrence of solo first ascents, the word "solo" in brackets follows their name.

This guidebook does not use a star rating system. Mixed routes are constantly changing from season to season and even ascent to ascent. They can form slightly different every year making it difficult to attach a subjective quality grade. Some routes that would be three-star classics like *Uniform Queen* on the Stanley Headwall and *Ten Years After* on Mount Rundle have only ever formed once making it irrelevant to assign a quality rating. Obviously, some routes are going to be better than others so the best way to find out which ones are the best is to go climb them. Ultimately, no star ratings also helps to avoid over-crowding on routes keeping the impact of tools and crampons to a minimum.

Mixed Grades

This guide uses primarily the M grade system to rate the difficulty of mixed routes. M grades were introduced by Jeff Lowe (the originator of WI grades as well) in the mid-'90s to combine rock and ice grades into one simple number to define the crux of a mixed route. Like any grading system, it has its drawbacks but seems to work fine. Traditionally, mixed routes were graded using both rock and waterfall grades (and aid grades when applicable).

The M system goes from M1 to M10 with M9+/M10- being the hardest in this book. There is an M11 in Europe but the European system seems to be inflated by one number grade. +'s and -'s are added to M grades to broaden the range and avoid compressing.

There will no doubt be inconsistencies with grades in this guidebook owing to the M grading system being relatively new. However, unlike pure rock climbing, and ice climbing to a lesser extent, mixed routes are constantly changing from year to year and even ascent to ascent. One cannot split hairs over grades because mixed routes are much more dynamic. A hold may break, the dagger could snap off, thin ice could melt, moss might get scrapped off; all of which make subsequent ascents harder.

The M grade is supposed to give you a general idea of what you are in store for and how hard you will have to "pull." It is only supposed to reflect technical difficulty regardless of whether the route is a 10 m over-bolted sport rig or a 5 pitch run out trad horror show. Undoubtedly, the later type of route of the same grade will "feel" much harder.

For routes that lack bomber gear protecting the crux, an R is placed after the grade. If maiming or even death occurs owing to a fall from the crux, then the route gets a big fat X by the technical grade. The X represents no gear at the crux but can also be associated with collapse potential of a hanging drip. Obviously, all free-hanging drips have the potential to snap off but some have more severe consequences than others.

Following is a comparison chart of M grades to Yosemite decimal system grades. This is to give you an idea of how strenuous a route should feel.

M4	5.8
M5	5.9
M6	5.10
M7	5.11
M8	5.11+/5.12
M9	5.12+/5.13-
M10	5.13

Some routes in this guide still have the traditional mixed grading system of a YDS rock grade and a WI grade. This is because either these routes are rarely done, therefore the newer M grade is not known, or it has a pure rock pitch that is usually climbed with hands. Some routes also have aid grades (A0 to A3). A0 meaning the route has a point of aid or a rest on the rope was taken. A3 indicates a substantial length of hard artificial climbing. Modern dry tooling has essentially made aid on mixed routes obsolete, however, a few routes still have some aid sections that will undoubtedly go free.

This book also uses a commitment grade that is the same for waterfall ice routes in the Canadian Rockies. It is not comparable to rock, big wall or alpine commitment grades. It gives the climber an idea of how engaging a route is and what severity of objective hazards to expect.

Commitment grade uses Roman numerals from I to VI. The only VI in the book is *Rocket Man* on Mount Patterson because of its high altitude, alpine nature; exposure to seracs and avalanches on the approach; and its overall length. Cragging, sport-style mixed routes get no commit grade but could still have objective hazards above or on the approach, like the Gulag.

Gear

The amount and type of gear required for the routes described in this book vary hugely from climb to climb. Some of the short sport-style rigs only call for quick draws, not even screws, while other traditional routes require beefy rock racks. For routes that take gear other than quick draws for bolts and screws, a gear section is included in the route description detailing what is needed. Most call for a "standard mixed rack," which consists of the following:

> Half dozen pitons including knife-blades (KBs), lost arrows (LAs) and angles.
> Set of nuts.
> TCUs and cams to 3" or 3.5".
> Selection of smaller Tri-cams.
> Ice hook.
> Ice screws, usually including stubby ice screws as well.
> Long slings for threading icicles, or chockstones.

Some routes require more gear, which is noted. All climbers have their favourite and preferred types of equipment. Many will not bother with the ice hook for instance, while others swear by them for pounding into icy cracks or frozen moss.

Be leery of fixed gear like pitons, which can loosen from the effects of melt-freeze (see Hazards).

60 m ropes have become the norm and many routes require them for descending. One rope will usually suffice for most single-pitch cragging routes. Two ropes are required for most of the multi-pitch climbs, mainly for getting off. Double 8.5 mm or 9 mm are nice for traditional routes that wander a bit as they help eliminate dreaded rope drag.

Avalanches

The Canadian Rockies is avalanche country. The Great White Wave threatens about half of the routes described in this book. Hardly anyone dies in the Rockies from difficulties encountered on routes; many die from avalanches though! Most ice and mixed routes naturally lie under gullies and bowls that accumulate with snow ready to be triggered. The Banff Park Warden office (403-762-1460) has a recorded avalanche bulletin that is updated daily. If the hazard is considerable or higher, then consider safer climbing venues. Even if the posting is moderate, it doesn't mean avalanches are impossible. Always keep a heads up for potentially dangerous situations like steep approach slopes, wind-loaded gullies and sun-baked bowls. Be versed in avalanche safety procedures by reading books and taking courses. A good book is *Avalanche Safety for Climbers, Skiers & Snowboarders* by Tony Daffern. Yamnuska Mountain School (403-678-4164) and many local guiding agencies offer avalanche courses. For routes with major slopes leading up to them, carry a beacon and shovel just in case and know how to use them.

Routes that have low avalanche hazard:

> Balfour Wall, The
> *Bookworm*
> *Bullwinkle*
> *Captain Hook*
> Cline River Gallery
> *Dead Eye Dick*
> *End Of Days*
> Hammer Horror area (unless very high snowfall)
> *Fire Drake*
> *Forgotten Land*
> Ghost area

Grassi Lakes
Grotto Canyon
Gunfighter, The
Haffner Creek
Kicking Horse Canyon routes
(except *Jacob's Ladder*)
Lessons of Oka
Magic Touch
Marble Canyon
Margaritaville
Mixed Master
Mr. Hankey
Naked Gun
Opal Creek routes (*Red Man Soars*, *Hovering Half Breed*, *Green Man Gronks*)
Pipimenchen
Rock On and Off
Snowbird
Waterfowl Gullies (unless very high snowfall)

Other Hazards

Other than avalanches, there are many other hazards that can pose a threat to mixed climbers.

Beware of frigid arctic fronts that cause skinny pillars and hanging daggers to suddenly collapse. Extreme cold weather is also prime conditions for frostbite and hypothermia.

Pay close attention to suspect rock. Loose choss that was at one time frozen in place may have defrosted. Ice tools exert an inordinate amount of force when levered behind blocks and flakes. Prying a huge chunk of limestone onto yourself or onto your belayer's head would be a bad thing. Even pulling off small rocks from a mixed pitch can injure your belayer or chop your ropes.

More committing backcountry climbs that are far from the road or off the beaten track should be treated as "full-on" undertakings. Remote or semi-alpine routes can take all day to approach, climb and descend, so a party must be prepared with headlamps, belay jackets, extra food and water, and a first-aid kit. Getting rappel ropes stuck or getting lost in the dark are sure ways to spend a cold winter night out in the open.

Thin creek ice in areas like Marble Canyon, Haffner Creek and Cline River gallery can be an accident waiting to happen. Watch where you are walking so you do not punch through a thin section and get flushed away with the rushing river underneath.

Finally, fixed gear on mixed routes can be considered a hazard. The effects of the melt-freeze process can drastically weaken a once bomber fixed pin. Never trust a fixed pin without first testing it to insure its integrity. Some routes like *Red Man Soars* and *Shampoo Planet* are riddled with in situ pitons. This takes some of the sting out of the climbing but do not treat them like their bolted brethren. Be prepared to reset fixed gear or place your own pins.

Environmental Considerations

There are a few considerations climbers must acknowledge with regard to the environment they play in. Climbing in general and mixed climbing specifically can have a lasting negative affect on the crags.

Please stay off established summer sport routes. Ice axes and crampons not only scratch the rock but can also destroy holds on a rock climb. If you want to train on rock then find some scrappy, undeveloped crag (the Rockies have an unlimited supply) to tool around on.

Climbers have a huge impact on the places they frequent. Some of the more popular cragging areas like Haffner Creek require winter climbers to be responsible. This means walking out of the canyon and away from the creek to defecate and urinate. There are toilets at the parking area that should be used before approaching. Yellow stains greatly affect the aesthetics and sanitation of these areas. Please do not urinate anywhere near routes as it stinks and is visually unappealing.

Style

A climber's style plays an important role in how long a mixed route will last during a season. Heavy handed swinging will destroy fragile ice features that might make a route doable. Uncontrolled wailing at ice daggers will only result in them breaking and you falling. If you get too pumped and can't stay in control, then find easier routes to do until you get stronger or acquire more subtle technique. The same goes for footwork. Try to control your feet from skating around all over the place and scratching the rock more than necessary.

On a final note, if the temperature is too warm, refrain from getting on established mixed routes. Trying to push the season will only result in broken holds and trashed moss.

New Routes

The Canadian Rockies has incredible potential for new mixed routes. The possibilities are endless for both huge, multi-pitch adventures and short, technical testpieces. No doubt this guidebook will entice more people to get out there looking for that ultimate mixed line. There are a few considerations to keep in mind when establishing first ascents.

On traditional mixed routes, anything goes including fixed pins, gear and, of course, no gear. If placing bolts though, please try to use stainless steel bolts in conjunction with a stainless steel hanger. These should be no less than 3/8" in diameter and 3" or more in length. Regular steel bolts rust very quickly owing to their exposure to intense moisture that is present on most mixed climbs all year. The cheap and easy "self drive" bolt is commonly used throughout the Rockies. Though fast to place, they are also quick to degrade because of the multitude of different metals involved. "Self drive" bolts are great as an emergency bolt kit, but if you are planning on developing new routes please take the responsibility to place high quality stainless steel expansion bolts.

If you are putting up a sport-style mixed rig at a popular or soon-to-be popular cragging venue, use 3/8" by 3" or 3 1/2" stainless steel expansion bolts. Anything less is unacceptable.

If a new route is not climbed free, please record it as such with its relative aid grade. If you are going to leave aid on a new route, be prepared for subsequent ascents to eliminate it thus claiming the first free ascent. On cragging-style routes, a new route is not complete until it has been climbed "redpoint" to the anchors without hanging on the rope like in sport rock climbing.

If you climb a new route, please record the following:

- A description of the exact location including detailed directions for the access and approach; map references if it is in an obscure area.

- Name of the climb.

- Grade of the climb including commitment grade, technical grade and seriousness grade (if applicable).

- Length of the whole route in metres.

- Date and names of first ascensionists.

- Gear list.

- If it is a multi-pitch route, provide pitch descriptions including individual pitch grades and lengths as well as belay anchor information (i.e., bolts, fixed pitons or exact gear required to build an anchor).

- Descent details whether it be by rappel or walk off.

- If possible, include a drawn topo of the route mapping out each pitch similar to the ones in this book.

Send new route information to:
Sean Isaac
c/o Rocky Mountain Books
4 Spruce Centre SW
Calgary, Alberta
T3C 3B3 Canada

or email descriptions to:
mixedguide@hotmail.com

or use the Outdoors Forum at **www.rmbooks.com**

Any corrections (there are bound to be a few) can also be forwarded to my attention at the above mailing address and email address.

Civilization

Canmore and Banff have all the amenities that a winter climber desires. Both are thriving towns with numerous great restaurants and bars, gear shops, climbing gyms and recreation centres.

For cheap accommodation, the Alpine Club of Canada Clubhouse (403-678-3200) on Indian Flats Road provides dormitory style rooms for $15 if you are a member and $21 if not. It has a large shared kitchen, sauna, laundry facilities, drying room and a great climbing library. Another option, with similar facilities, is the Banff International Hostel (403-762-4122) on Tunnel Mountain Road, which offers bunks for $20 for members and $24 for nonmembers.

Good greasy spoon breakfasts are served at Craig's Way Station on Highway 1A in Canmore and Banff Avenue in Banff. For coffee and great bagel breakfasts head to Rocky Mountain Bagel Company (403-678-9978) with two locations in Canmore: one on Main Street (8th Avenue) and one on Bow Valley Trail (Highway 1A). Both open at 6:30 am. The one on Main Street (open until 11 pm) also doubles as a book and magazine shop creating a mellow place to hang out. If you are climbing around Lake Louise, don't forget Laggen's Deli for bakery treats and day olds. "Apres" climbing beer and food can be found at the Grizzly Paw or The Drake in Canmore or one of the many bars and restaurants that line the main street in Banff.

There many excellent gear shops around that stock everything a mixed climber needs. Mountain Magic Equipment (403-762-2591) located on Bear Street in Banff has the biggest and best selection. The knowledgeable staff are also usually abreast of local route conditions. In Canmore, both Valhalla Pure Outfitters (403-678-5610) and Altitude Sports (403-678-1636) on 8th Street (Main Street) carry climbing equipment.

If you are worried about getting soft "glove hands" or still have lots of energy after a day of mixed climbing, check out the Rock Gardens (403-609-0101) at 109 Boulder Crescent in the industrial area behind the RCMP station in Canmore. This is an awesome bouldering gym that will guarantee a brutal pump.

On rest days, soak in the Banff Upper Hot Springs (403-762-1515) for $7; open from 10 am to 10 pm (11 pm on Fridays and Saturdays) every day. The Canmore Recreation Centre (403-678-5597) has a weight room, pool, hot tub and sauna for less than $4. Both Banff and Canmore have libraries with good climbing sections to keep you entertained. Downhill, Nordic and backcountry skiing are also good options to break up the climbing routine.

Glossary

Abalakov: Also know as a V-Thread or Ice Hourglass. A rappel anchor constructed by drilling and removing two long ice screws at a 45 degree angle to each other so they create a V through the ice. A 50 to 100 cm length of 7 mm cord is then treaded into one hole and fished out the other one by using a 30 cm length of coat hanger wire with a hooked bend on one end. Commercial "Abalakov Hookers" are sold specifically for this purpose. The cord is tied thus creating a bomber rap anchor.

Adze: A sharp attachment for ice tools designed to chop ice but have little use in mixed climbing except for the rare instance the adze will jam in a crack. It is also the perfect implement for an instant lobotomy, if your tool happens to pop and smack you in the forehead.

Bolt: 3" to 3 1/2" of 3/8" stainless steel placed in a drilled hole and used for protection. Usually represented by the ubiquitous "X" on topos. Self drives, quarter inchers and fixed pins are all known impostors.

Choss: Overly shattered limestone that is synonymous with the Canadian Rockies. The yellow variety is particularly rank.

Dagger: A free hanging "goatee" of ice that does not touch the ground. These icicles are inherently under much tension and have enormous potential for collapse. Approach with caution.

Drip: See **Dagger**.

Drooling: A term coined for dry tooling rock to reach unformed icicles.

Dry Tooling: 1. "Something we used to do in high school when we couldn't get a date for the weekend." 2. Utilizing ice tools on rock holds instead of hands to gain upward progress.

Figure 4: A contrived yet effective technique accomplished by hooking a leg over the opposite arm thus increasing reach without having to lock off.

Figure 9: Similar to a Figure 4 except that same leg over same arm.

Ice Hook: A medieval looking device originally designed as pound-in thin ice protection but works better in frozen moss/dirt and ice glazed, chossy cracks.

Lever: See **Stein Puller**.

Manky: Protection, usually fixed, that is less than desirable, i.e., He was afraid to even breathe on the manky pin for fear of it falling out.

Scumming: A technique by which various body parts are pasted to rock or ice features and the resulting friction from the clothing material and surface area allows purchase to be gained, i.e., butt scum, knee scum, hip scum, shoulder scum, etc.

Shaft Jam: Placing the shaft of your tool horizontally into a crack then grabbing and pulling down just below the head to create leverage.

Stien Puller: Placing your pick on a dry tool hold then pulling back on the shaft so the head of the tool is braced solidly on rock hence locking the tool in place with two opposing points of contact.

Stubbies: 10 cm ice screws.

Torquing: Twisting the picks of your tools in a crack to gain purchase.

Turf: Frozen moss, grass or dirt that will accept solid pick placements. Popularized in Scotland, turf climbing is a form of mixed climbing in which ice is not necessarily required.

Will Gadd dynoing on Money for Nothing and Your Picks for Free. *Photo Gadd collection.*

Despite almost 40 waterfall routes, Waterton only hosts a single mixed climb. Undoubtedly, there is huge potential but it has yet to be tapped. The area suffers greatly from the effects of chinooks causing routes to melt out prematurely.

The Deviant II 5.6 WI5, 35 m

Approach From the Waterton townsite, drive up Cameron Lake Road for 4 km and park just past the creekbed that descends from *Quick and Dirty* (WI3, 80 m). Hike along the left side of the creek through trees to the amphitheatre (82 H/4 854391). *The Deviant* is found 5 m right of *Quick and Dirty* and is identified as a broad curtain of ice pouring from a ledge about 30 m up.

Gear Standard mixed rack.

A thin smear leads steeply to a rock roof (fixed pin). Traverse right on big, incut holds and good gear to the ice ledge. Belay on screws.

Descent Rappel from Abalakov.

Joe Josephson on the first ascent of The Deviant. *Photo Brad Wrobleski.*

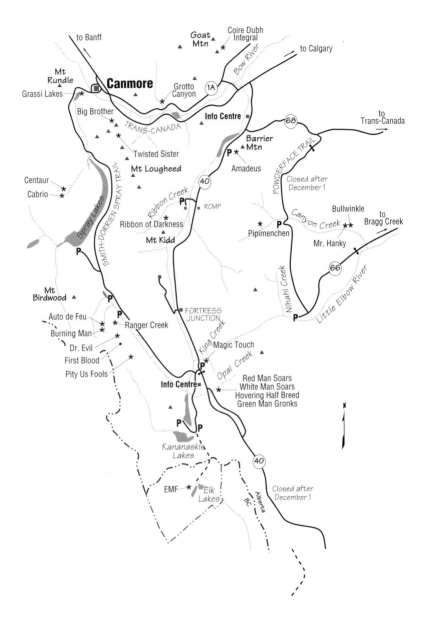

to Banff

Goat Mtn

Coire Dubh Integral

to Calgary

Bow River

Mt Rundle

Canmore

Grotto Canyon

1A

Grassi Lakes

Info Centre

to Trans-Canada

68

Big Brother

TRANS-CANADA

Barrier Mtn

POWDERFACE TRAIL

Twisted Sister

P

Mt Lougheed

Amadeus

Closed after December 1

Centaur

SMITH-DORRIEN SPRAY TRAIL

40

Ribbon Creek

Bullwinkle

to Bragg Creek

Cabrio

P

Canyon Creek

RCMP

Pipimenchen

Mr. Hanky

Spray Lakes

Ribbon of Darkness

Mt Kidd

66

P

Nihahi Creek

Little Elbow River

Mt Birdwood

P

P

FORTRESS JUNCTION

Auto de Feu

P

Ranger Creek

King Creek

Magic Touch

Burning Man

Dr. Evil

Opal Creek

First Blood

P

Pity Us Fools

Info Centre

Red Man Soars
White Man Soars
Hovering Half Breed
Green Man Gronks

P

P

Kananaskis Lakes

40

EMF

Elk Lakes

Alberta BC

Closed after December 1

N

Canyon Creek

These are probably the closest two mixed routes to Calgary. They used to be even closer before the Canyon Creek road was closed.

Approach From the four-way stop on the outskirts of Bragg Creek, take Highway 22 south for 3.5 km to the junction with SR 66. Turn right (west) and follow SR 66 for 16 km to Canyon Creek. Cross the bridge and take the next right, opposite the Elbow River boat launch. Park 600 m down at Ing's Mine trailhead. The road used to continue farther along but is now closed and this seems to be permanent. A 30 minute bike ride takes you to the "old" Ing's Mine parking area. Walk north up Moose Dome Creek toward the Shell gas plant. Just before the top of the first hill, go northwest through the trees and up to the base of the following two routes (82 J/15 550416).

A Bullwinkle II 5.10 WI4+, 90 m

1) 5.10-, 45 m. Begin right of the main ice. Climb loose rock (fixed pin) to a short left-facing corner (crux) and continue up blocky terrain trending left to a two bolt anchor on a ledge just right of the upper ice.

2) WI4+/5, 45 m. The bottom of the pillar may be thin but thickens higher up. Belay at the blocks on top (fixed pin).

Descent Rappel from a tree out right to the two bolt anchor, then to the ground. Double ropes required.

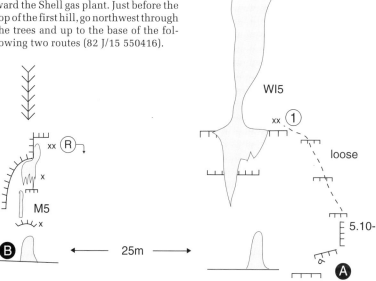

B Mr. Hanky II M6, 30 m

Located 25 m left of *Bullwinkle* is a prominent iced up right-facing corner. Climb a short smear to an awkward alcove. Clip a bolt on the right and pull into the vein of ice above. Climb this to below some icicles and traverse right to a bolt. Make some dry tool moves to reach more ice in a short right-facing corner and follow it to a bolt belay on the right below a large roof.

Gear Standard mixed rack.

Pipimenchen 5.6 A1 WI4, 90 m

Approach Continue past Canyon Creek to Powderface Trail. Follow Powderface Trail (closed after Dec. 1) for 14 km to a sharp curve at the bottom of a hill. Park here. Hike an hour up Canyon Creek to where the route can be seen in the first small cirque on the right (north). It is 20 more minutes to the base (map reference: 82 J/15 431404). If driving from Canmore, take Highway 40 to SR 68 (Sibbald Creek Trail), which is followed for 14 km to Powderface Trail. Turn right and drive south for 20 km. Park at the same sharp curve as mentioned above.

Gear Standard mixed rack.

1) 5.6 A1, 50 m. Located 30 m to the left of the icicle is a shallow groove of waterworn rock. Aid the groove using five bolts and gear for 20 m, then traverse up and right (5.4 R) to a two bolt anchor just left of the ice. This pitch is equipped and ready for an all free ascent.

2) WI4, 50 m. Straightforward ice to the top. Belay from the trees.

Descent Rappel the route first from a tree at the top then from the two bolt anchor at the end of pitch 1.

Mr. Hanky *left and* Bullwinkle *right. Photo Ralph Slawinski.*

First ascent of Pipimenchen. *Photo Jeff Everett.*

Barrier Mountain

Amadeus III 5.9 (M5) WI4, 70 m

A great early season route that usually melts out after the first chinook. It rarely forms as an ice route but comes in as a mixed climb every year. A direct start straight up to the hanging dagger has been climbed on very bad gear. The regular mixed variation traverses in from the right and is fairly well protected.

Approach Park on the east side of Highway 40, 4.7 km south of the Barrier Lake Visitor Centre. A good summer trail heads through the woods and into a drainage that is followed up steep, compact scree to the base of the route. 1 hour.

Gear Standard mixed rack.

1) 5.9 (M5) WI4, 30 m. From a rock belay (one bolt and cams) high on the right side below a rock chimney, climb a shallow rock grove out left for a few metres, then traverse left into a corner. Get some good gear before belly flopping onto the water-polished slab. Grovel up onto your knees and eventually your feet, then traverse left again to the ice (run out), which is climbed to a shelter belay on the left of the upper pillar.

2) WI4, 40 m. Climb ice to the top.

Descent Double rope 60 m rap to the ground.

Amadeus *in typical condition.*
Photo *Rob Owens.*

Ribbon Creek

Ribbon of Darkness III 5.7 WI5, 50 m

Named after a Gordon Lightfoot song, *Ribbon of Darkness* is located on the north face of Mount Kidd. A long approach for a short route.

Approach From the Trans-Canada Highway take Highway 40 to Kananaskis Village, then follow signs to Ribbon Creek parking area. Ski groomed trails heading up Ribbon Creek. When the trails end, continue up the valley until the route is visible high on the left side at the top of a 300 m slope (map reference: 82 J/14 405265). Major avalanche potential.

Gear Half dozen pitons (mainly KBs) and ice screws.

Make a rising traverse right on rotten rock (5.7) to reach the hanging icicle.

Descent Rappel the route with double ropes from an Abalakov.

Jeff Everett on Ribbon of Darkness.
Photos Dave Campbell (top)
Glen Reisenhofer (bottom).

King Creek

Magic Touch II WI3 R 5.8, 50 m

Approach Park on the side of Highway 40 at King Creek (signed) near the junction with Kananaskis Lakes Road. Hike up the canyon for 20 minutes. The route is on the right side just before the King Creek ice flows.

Gear Standard mixed rack.

1) WI3 R M3, 25 m. A thin sheet of ice finishes in a mixed traverse right around a small roof to a belay stance (fixed piton and natural gear) on a ledge.

2) 5.8, 25 m. Straight above the belay climb a 3" crack that narrows toward the top offering good gear all the way. A two bolt station is on a ledge to the left.

Descent Rappel the route from the two bolt station with double 50 m ropes.

Shawn Huisman and Jamie McVickers on pitch 2 of Magic Touch. *Photo Shelly Huisman.*

Opal Creek

The drips and smears surrounding *Whiteman Falls* (WI6) offer high quality, traditional mixed climbing.

Approach From the Trans-Canada, drive 54 km south on Highway 40 to the Kananaskis Lakes Trail junction. After December 1, Highway 40 is closed beyond here so you must walk/ski for 5 km to Valley View Road. Before December 1, drive to this point and park here. Hike along the road past a gate to the creek on the left. Follow the creek past two tiers of WI3 (may not be frozen early in the season) and up the canyon to Whiteman Falls and the following four mixed routes.

Red Man Soars III 5.10- WI4+ (M5+), 55 m

Classic mixed climbing with tons of fixed gear. Climb up a verglassed corner, step left on to the arete for a few moves, and then back right to gain the ice. Possible belay in chimney off of ice screws. A direct variation to the first pitch climbs thin ice and mixed rock to the right of the regular start to reach the curtain straight on. The second pitch continues up the chimney for more thin ice and mixed rock moves to a fixed anchor in an alcove from which the ice flows.

Gear Standard mixed rack.

Descent A double 55 m rope rappel from the fixed anchor at the top will reach the ground.

Red Man Soars. *Photo Dave Campbell.*

White Man Soars III 5.9+ R WI6 (M6+ R), 55 m

The mixed connector pitch joining the top of *Red Man Soars* to *Whiteman Falls.* Traverse up and left on poor rock to a blob of ice, then continue the traverse to reach the fat ice of *Whiteman Falls.* If the ice half way across the traverse is not thick enough for screws, then the pitch gets an X rating because rock gear potential is minimal.

Gear KBs and screws (if you're lucky).

Descent Rappel from the two bolt anchor on the right side at the top of Whiteman Falls.

Hovering Half Breed M7+, 30 m

A sport mixed pitch between *Whiteman Falls* and *Red Man Soars*. The lower ice apron of Whiteman Falls leads to the first bolt, then follow a right-facing, right-arching corner past many bolts and fixed pins to a two bolt lower-off anchor. Sometimes ice smears will be present weeping from the arching overlap but usually it is dry.

Green Man Gronks III 5.9 M6, 45 m

An obvious verglassed chimney about 50 m downhill from *Whiteman Falls* on the left side (looking up hill). A splitter crack running the length of the route provides great protection. Begin by jamming a hand crack in a right-facing corner, then squirm into the chimney and squeeze to the top.

Gear Standard mixed rack with double cams from 2" to 4".

Descent Rappel from single bolt.

Green Man Gronks.
Photo Sean Isaac.

Elk Lakes

EMF IV A0 WI6, 120 m

Located left of *Elk Tear* (WI5) is a discontinuous smear with a short rock section in the middle. The crux still awaits a proper free ascent.

Approach From Highway 40, take the Kananaskis Lake Trail for 12 km to the Elk Pass parking area. Ski up Fox Creek to Elk Pass then follow the power line south to the summer hiking trail that ascends to Upper Elk Lake. *EMF* and the other ice climbs are found across the lake on the south face of Mount Fox.

1) WI4, 45 m. An easy ice gully leads to a short pillar. Belay from screws at the base of a steep section of unconsolidated icicles.

EMF *is the smear on the left. Photo Dave Campbell.*

Dave Campbell leading pitch 3 of EMF. *Photo Glen Reisenhofer.*

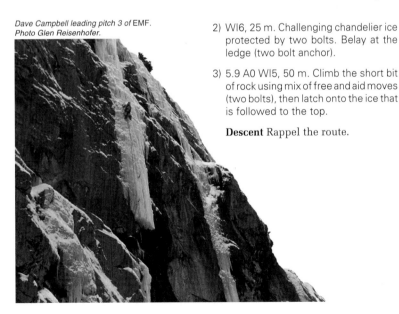

2) WI6, 25 m. Challenging chandelier ice protected by two bolts. Belay at the ledge (two bolt anchor).

3) 5.9 A0 WI5, 50 m. Climb the short bit of rock using mix of free and aid moves (two bolts), then latch onto the ice that is followed to the top.

Descent Rappel the route.

Centaur *left and* Cabrio *right. Photo Grant Statham.*

Goat Glacier

Two parallel ice runnels form near the edge of the Goat Glacier. Both are long aesthetic lines that form early season.

Approach Just south of the Spray Lakes Ranger Station on the Smith-Dorrien Road, cross the dam and drive 1 km down the west shore of the lake. Park at a campsite (map reference: 82J/14 149493) and head up the creek for two hours to the two climbs (100 m apart) on the right side of the valley at the toe of the Goat Glacier. Avalanche hazard will increase drastically as snow accumulates.

Cabrio IV WI5 R, 400 m

This is the right-hand of the two runnels. It is a thin ice route requiring mixed protection. In fatter years, it would be a pure ice route. The first half of the route can be super thin (read: 1 cm thick ice), but the upper part is much easier.

Gear 10 pitons, half set of nuts, screws including stubbies.

Descent Rappel route from Abalakovs and rock anchors.

Centaur IV 5.9 WI4, 350 m

This is the left-hand flow that does not touch down.

Gear Standard mixed rack.

60 m right of the main ice floe is a 50 m corner system that leads to a ledge. Make a rock anchor at the top of the ledge then traverse left to the ice and up to a two bolt anchor. Continue up thicker and easier ice for 250 m to the top.

Descent Rappel the upper route from Abalakovs to the two bolt anchor at top of pitch 2. From here, continue straight down the drainage to a rock anchor (nuts and hexes) on the right of the ice. A final rap will reach the ground.

French Creek

Approach Park at Burstall Pass parking lot 45 km from Canmore along the Smith-Dorrien Road. Hike or ski across the flats and up the first hill taking the left-hand fork when the road splits. Follow this up into French Creek with the routes on the right. 1.5 hours.

Auto de Feu IV M6 WI5 R, 300 m

A series of discontinuous smears adorn the right-hand wall of the valley. *Auto de Feu* is the first one you come to.

Gear Half dozen pins, tri-cams, screws.

Steepening ice to a WI5 pillar. Belay at top on ice. Follow the gully above up snow and short sections of ice (WI3 and 4) to a short rock wall with a hole in it. Tunnel through the hole, then wander 25 m up the gully to a belay in a rock cave below the final ice. For the last pitch (crux), climb ice-splattered rock on the right for 5 m

then step left to 10 m of ice ending in an alcove. Dry tool rock and moss for 5 m (M6) to gain an "anemic curtain" in a groove. In total, the last pitch is 30 m. Fixed pin belay is on the right.

Descent Rappel the route.

Burning Man IV M6 WI5, 300 m

Located 250 m left of *Auto de Feu* is a thin ice route named *Coffee Sucking Do Nothings* (IV WI4, 220 m). The start of *Burning Man* is accessed by climbing the first pitch of this route then traversing left on an easy snow ledge.

Gear Few pins, screws and stubbies.

Climb grade three ice on the first pitch of *Coffee Sucking Do Nothings*, then walk up snow to the bottom of the next steep ice section. Traverse a snow ledge left to belay below the hanging icicle of *Burning Man*. 5 m of rock (one bolt) gains the unformed ice. Continue for three more pitches of ice up to WI4+.

Descent Rappel the route from Abalakovs then reverse the traverse back over to *Coffee Sucking Do Nothings*.

A. Burning Man, *B.* Auto de Feu. *Photo Joe Josephson.*

Ranger Creek

Ranger Creek is home to some of the earliest formed ice every season. For this reason, it's very popular with eager October climbers; thus, every drip and smear has felt the whack of picks making it hard to decipher who has climbed what. The following two routes are definitely the best mixed lines in this drainage though numerous others can be found. Ranger Creek should be avoided after the heavy snows of winter set in because it is surrounded by major avalanche terrain.

Approach Park at the gated road on the west side of the Smith-Dorrien Spray Trail, 5 km past Burstall Pass. The ice route, *R&D* (WI4), will be visible on the left side of the Ranger Creek bowl. From the parking area, drop down the embankment then hike up and left through alders into the creekbed. Follow this to the treeline then hike up the avalanche prone slopes to *Plastic Exploding Universe* on the left wall or continue another 30 minutes to *Thin Universe* at the back of the bowl. 45 minutes to 1.5 hours.

Plastic Exploding Universe M7 WI5, 60 m

Gear Standard mixed rack.

Begin climbing low angle rock 10 m to the right of *R&D*, following a series of discontinuous cracks and flake systems via thin dry tooling. A possible belay (mid-size cams) at a small stance on the left can be construed. From this spot, traverse a bit right and climb over a bulge (M7) to a steep continuous crack system (very thin ice) and eventually the last few metres of *R&D*. A two bolt belay can be found on the back wall. It is possible to do as one very long pitch.

Descent Rappel *R&D* from the two bolt anchor on the back wall.

Thin Universe   M7 WI4 R, 40 m

This is the anaemic dribble of ice that pours over the steep cliff left of *Lone Ranger* (WI3). The first attempt resulted in a dramatic fall when the curtain of ice snapped sending the leader for a huge ride. A hard route that forms every year.

Gear Standard mixed rack.

Begin right of the anaemic dribble and trend left toward it over very steep rock. Finding good gear is challenging but at least a bolt protects the final moves onto the thin, detached ice.

South Kananaskis Lakes

Dr. Evil IV 5.6 WI5 R, 75 m

An early season route located in the bowl to the north of *First Blood* (WI5) and on the same rock band as that climb. A number of lines are easily visible from the road with *Dr. Evil* being the leftmost route identified as a series of discontinuous smears leading up to an ice hose.

Approach Park on the side of the Smith-Dorrien Road 5 km south of Burstall Pass. Bushwhack through alders into the drainage below the route and follow open slopes to the base. 2.5 hours. The route forms very early in the season, and would be suicidal with any avalanche hazard.

Gear Half dozen pitons (KBs to angles), ice screws including stubbies.

1) 5.6 WI5 R, 30 m. Begin at a single bolt anchor on a sloping snow ledge accessed by traversing in from the right. Move left to a short curtain. Climb it, then move right and up over easy but loose rock to the base of a short, freestanding icicle (bolt). Climb the icicle to a belay behind the upper pillar (piton).

2) WI5, 45 m. Climb the short freestanding pillar and the ice hose above to a two bolt belay on the right.

Descent Rappel the route with double 60 m ropes to reach the ground.

Pity us Fools IV 5.7 WI5+, 70 m

Pity us Fools (map reference: 82 J/11 203225) isn't visible from the road but is in the second, large bowl to the left of *First Blood*. This is a cold area ensuring that this route will come in early every year. There is considerable exposure to avalanches on the approach. The name reflects the four hour epic bushwhack that ensued from a wrong turn during the approach on the first ascent.

Approach Park 6.2 km south of the Burstall Pass parking lot just beyond the junction with James Walker Creek (signed). Head up the obvious drainage on the west side of the road, which is the Murray Creek drainage. Follow (skis) the drainage into the cirque and the route will become visible in the far right-hand side of the cirque. Negotiate potential avalanche terrain to the base of the route. 2 hours.

Gear Screws including stubbies, half dozen pitons.

1) 5.7 WI3, 30 m. Thin ice and easy mixed lead to a snow ledge. Belay on screws.

2) WI5+, 40 m. Steep chandelier ice.

Descent Rappel the route.

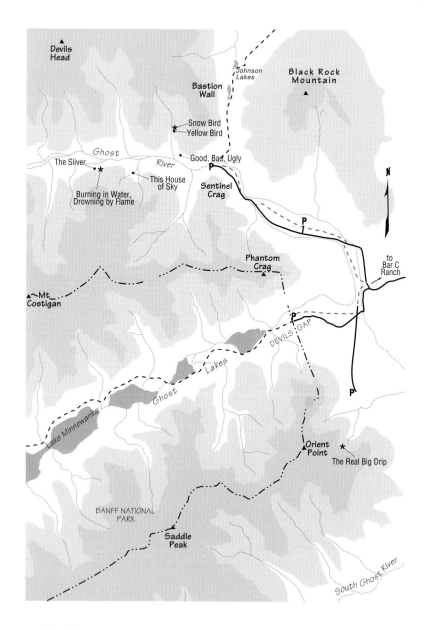

THE GHOST

The Ghost is a wild place guaranteed to serve up epic adventure. Huge walls of limestone and big remote climbs are the mainstay. Needless to say, there is a lot more potential for mixed climbing here than the few routes described below. Be warned though, a 4x4 vehicle with high suspension (read: truck) is recommended for winter outings in the Ghost. Decaying dirt roads, big boulders and car-devouring snow drifts are all standard fair. Avalanche danger is usually quite low in this area owing to the snow-eating effects of chinooks and high winds. This does not mean avalanches are nonexistent, especially during times of high snowfall.

The Ghost is accessed by following the Highway 1A from Canmore to SR 940 just east of the Ghost Reservoir. Drive along 940 for 22.7 km to a gated road on the left slightly beyond Richards Road. Close the cattle gate behind you. Follow the pot-holed dirt road for about 16 km to the top of the Big Hill that looks down onto the Ghost.

The Real Big Drip V M7+ WI7, 200 m

The Real Big Drip is the route that the *Big Drip* always wanted to be. No contrived (all mixed climbing is contrived anyway) traverse in from the side or hokey rapping in from the top. This is the full, from the ground, in-your-face, straight-up-the-guts version. An incredible line in an even more incredible setting.

Approach Easily visible from the top of the Big Hill in a large cirque to the southwest. Descend the Big Hill, cross a dry riverbed and drive about 3 km south, gradually gaining the west side of the valley bottom. Stop at an obvious cut line that goes steeply up on the right (west). Hike up the cut line for 10 minutes (1 km), then bushwhack south (left) through open pine forest to the creek. Climb above the south bank of the creek where it is intersected by a well-used horse trail. As the trail levels out at the top of the terrace it splits in two. Follow the right fork and then as the trail fades in the forest look for red flagging tape that will lead into the cirque. Finally, scramble up easy rock bands to the base of the climb. 1.5 hours.

1) M7 WI6+, 40 m. Dry tool past 15 bolts to a rest behind the hanging drip. Pull onto the ice and climb 15 m of steep, roofy ice to a two bolt belay on an ice ledge below a small roof. The ice pillar can be fragile and has collapse potential. Double ropes will help alleviate rope drag.

2) WI6/7, 30 m. Move left from the belay and climb interesting ice formations, finishing at a roomy ice ledge with a two bolt belay (may be covered by ice). On the first ascent, a WI7 mushroom roof presented the crux that may form differently in other years.

3) M7+, 30 m. Dry tool past 13 bolts to a small ice cave behind the dagger (two bolt belay). The crux is a small roof low down but the climbing is technical and sustained.

4) WI5, 40 m. Climb steep ice, then continue over easy ground to a small cave behind a curtain above the large halfway ledge.

5) WI4, 40 m. Steep, straightforward ice.

6) WI3, 30 m. Climb easy ice to the top.

Descent Rappel the route from Abalakovs and bolt anchors.

The Real Big Drip. Photo Dave Thomson.

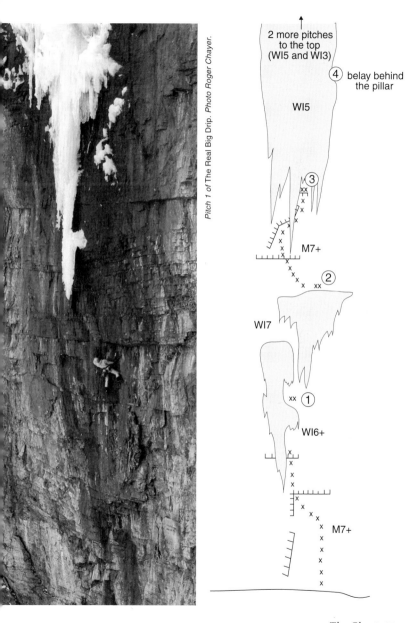

Pitch 1 of The Real Big Drip. *Photo Roger Chayer.*

2 more pitches
to the top
(WI5 and WI3)

④ belay behind
the pillar

WI5

③

M7+

②

WI7

① xx

WI6+

M7+

Raphael Slawinski on Burning in Water, Drowning by Flame. *Photo Rob Owens.*

Snowbird M6+, 40 m

Snowbird is located immediately left of *Yellow Bird* (WI4) in the Valley of the Birds. The line is a bit forced but fun nonetheless.

Approach From the bottom of the Big Hill turn right and follow rough roads into the North Ghost. With a 4x4 truck it is possible to drive right to the entrance to the Valley of the Birds. If driving a more meagre vehicle then park at an open gravel area about a 15 minute walk downstream of the valley entrance. Access to the valley is barred by a smooth, water polished slab. If there is ice, then it is easy; if not, then sketch up the rock with a fixed pin and bolt for protection. Follow the valley past short ice steps to a 20 m WI3 flow on the right. This is the first pitch of *Yellow Bird*. Climb it to reach the base of the second pitch of *Yellow Bird* and *Snowbird*.

Begin in a steep corner a couple metres left of *Yellow Bird*. An awkward section leads to an arete spattered with ice, then a ledge. Continue above the ledge past some thin, technical rock to a short ice curtain and eventually a tree belay.

Descent Double rope rappel from trees.

Burning in Water, Drowning by Flame M7, 30 m

Only known to form twice, this short yet burly testpiece involves hard climbing on suspect gear. The first ascensionists used a point of aid to reach out and snag the leftmost drip; however, the second and subsequent ascents dry tooled the committing roofs directly to gain the upper ice curtain.

Approach From the bottom of the Big Hill, turn right and follow rough roads into the North Ghost 2 km past GBU and the Valley of the Birds. If formed, there will be a noticeable low cliff band on the left. *The Sliver* is a WI6 pillar that forms about a 100 m to the right on the same cliff.

Gear Standard mixed rack.

From the top of the lower ice smear, power over the imposing roofs stuffing cams into loose horizontals to reach the upper ice.

Descent Rappel from Abalakov or walk off to the right.

Coire Dubh Intégral III 5.7 WI3, 550 m

Located on Goat Mountain, *Coire Dubh* is a rarely done 5.4 summer rock climb that becomes an excellent route in winter that should not be missed by aspiring mixed climbers. A classic multi-pitch adventure that even tops out on a summit (Loder Peak) for the full mountain experience. The constant wind and chinooks clear most of the white stuff off keeping avalanche hazard fairly low, but always be on the look out for isolated pockets of wind slab. It is best to keep clear after a big dump when the hazard will be at its worst and the rock climbing will feel more desperate.

Approach Park in a large pull-out on the south side of Highway 1A, 4.2 km east of the Exshaw bridge or 3.3 km west of the Seebe turn off (1A and 1X inter-

Coire Dubh Intégral. *Photo Joe Josephson.*

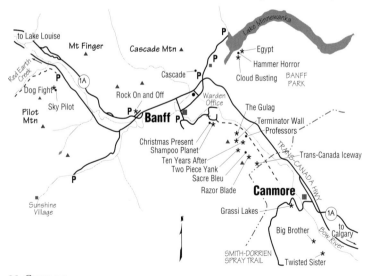

section). Cross the road and hike through the dump picking up a nice trail below Goat Mountain. Continue along the trail and through open forest to the creekbed that descends from the second major drainage on Goat Mountain. The first ice pitch will be obvious above in the gully.

The first pitch is WI3, then it kicks back and rambles up a gully opening into an amphitheatre. At this point, two options arise: 1. On the left, a thin ice groove with rock moves to finish (rarely enough ice); or 2. On the right, a left-facing pure rock corner with a bolt at the start to protect the crux moves. Above these obstacles, continue up on scree and third-class scrambling to a groove/gully on the right that is the only easy weakness in the wall above. Great pockets and thin

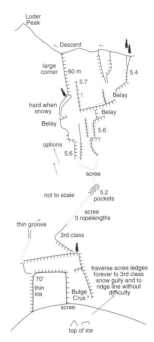

Twisted Sister is the line on the left. The right one is unclimbed. Photo Raphael Slawinski.

ice ascend through this feature depositing you below more scree and a variety of choices to finish. The main two variations are either straight up the snowy 5.6 groove/corner or the big left-facing dihedral (5.7) out left. Both offer fun climbing with good protection.

Descent Hike south over the top of Loder Peak and follow the ridge all the way to Highway 1A.

Twisted Sister IV 5.7 R WI4, 250 m

A fun early season route that can usually be climbed by early October. It is easily visible from the Trans-Canada Highway, high in Stewart Creek opposite (east) the Three Sisters.

Approach Park along the side of the Trans-Canada Highway 2.5 km west of the Three Sisters overpass or 2.5 km west of the Dead Man's Flat overpass. Hike through open forest and along dirt roads to gain Stewart Creek. Old mining roads and trails (some cairns) follow the valley bottom to the scree slope below the route. 2 to 3 hours. Approach is fine early season but gets harder as snow gets deeper. The slopes above and below pose an avalanche threat, but they are usually fine at the beginning of the season when snow is minimal.

1) 5.7 R, 45 m. Climb a low-angled right-trending groove to a small ledge, then continue up a steeper wall (bolt) to a fixed anchor just below a snow ledge.

2-4) WI2, 150 m. Climb three pitches of low-angled ice that snakes up a narrow gully.

5) WI4, 50 m. Steep ice leads to the top.

Descent Rappel the route.

Big Brother V M4 WI5 R/X, 200 m

Located on the north face of Little Sister, *Big Brother* sports thin ice mixed climbing in an alpine environment. An aesthetic line that is clearly visible from almost anywhere in Canmore.

Approach *Big Brother* is approached via Three Sisters Creek. Access to the creek is constantly changing owing to residential and commercial development in the Three Sisters area. From the Marriott Hotel, follow dirt roads along the power line to the creek. Hike up the creek avoiding a waterfall on the left via treed slopes. Continue up the drainage until below the First Sister, then head up steep trees to the scree below the face. Slog up snow gullies and scramble easy rock to the base of the route. 3 hours.

Gear Standard mixed rack.

A short step of ice leads to a snow slope in the gully and a rock belay on the left. The next step can have little or no ice in the corner (M4) making for sketchy climbing. Fixed rock belay on the right. Move the belay up the snow gully to the next steep section. A narrow ribbon of snowy ice ends at a one bolt anchor on the right at the base of the last pitch. Move left and climb a very thin smear for a long pitch past a detached pillar in the middle (crux) to a fixed rock anchor on the top on the left. Just before the pillar some good rock gear (small Tri-cams and/or 3/4" angle) can be arranged behind it to ease the runout.

Descent Rappel the route from fixed rock anchors.

Dion Bretzloff on Mental Jewelry. *Photo Sean Isaac.*

Grotto Canyon

Grotto Canyon was home to the first sport-style mixed route with the bolting of *Mental Jewelry*. Since then two other lines have been added to make this an easily accessible moderate mixed crag. No avalanche hazard.

Approach Park at the gravel lot on the north side of Highway 1A, 9.8 km east of the Trans-Canada overpass on the eastern edge of Canmore. The trail starts at the west end of the lot, crosses the tracks and heads through the woods to the mouth of the canyon. Follow the canyon to the fork and the ice routes, *His* and *Hers*. 30 minutes.

A Mental Jewelry M6+, 12 m
Begins immediately right of *His* (WI4; the left-hand ice pillar) and climb vertical rock past five bolts before swinging onto its right side.

B Sketch and Sniff M6+, 12 m
The three bolt mixed rig that begins left of *Hers* (WI4; the right-hand ice pillar) and joins it near the top.

C Secret Samadhi M5+, 12 m
Climbs rock to the right of *Hers* past four bolts and a 3"-3.5" cam placement between the second and third bolt. It also joins *Hers* but continues up to a higher set of anchors requiring a few more mixed moves.

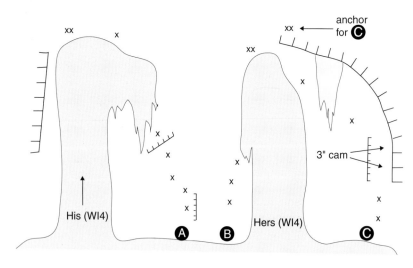

Grassi Lakes

Though a popular sport climbing area, Grassi Lakes ices up in the winter to produce some wet pillars (WI4) and a couple of fun bolted mixed lines on either side of the Hermit Wall. Please refrain from dry tooling on established summer sport routes.

Approach From the Canmore Nordic Centre, continue up the road to Whiteman's Pass between Ha Ling Peak (the mountain formally known as Chinaman's Peak) and EEOR (East End of Rundle). Do not park by the gated Trans Alta utility access road just above the canyon. Instead, park at a pull-out on the left side of the road about 300 m past the crest of the hill. Walk back along the road toward Canmore and descend into the canyon at the Trans Alta gate. The routes are on the right side and listed from right to left as you walk down the canyon.

The Overhang M6, 15 m

Just before the Hermit Wall, ice pours over a roof a few metres off the ground. The rock moves are protected by two bolts. After pulling the roof, easy ice ends at the trees.

Pascquala M6+, 20 m

Start at a ledge with a two bolt anchor half way up on the left side of the WI2 flow right of Hermit Wall. From the anchor, follow the obvious fault/crack that traverses left to the ice (six bolts). Sometimes the dagger touches down by the end of the season, which will make the transition from rock to ice easier.

Grant Statham on Double Dutch.
Photo Joe Josephson.

Double Dutch M7, 20 m

Located half way up the hill on the left side of Hermit Wall. Steep rock cranks out a small cave to a WI4 pillar (three bolts).

The Tyranny of Gear M7, 20 m

A natural gear route located immediately left of *Double Dutch*. Climb up to a small roof with a good crack (cams between 1" and 2") and pull onto a bit of ice. Move left across a pocketed wall and up a skinny pillar.

Descent All three routes can be descended by either rappelling from trees or walking easily down the far left or far right side.

MOUNT RUNDLE

Park Boundary

Trans-Canada Iceway
IV M5 WI4 R, 180 m

A semi-alpine ice runnel high on Mount Rundle. It is more of a thin ice route as it does not have any real dry tooling, but it definitely requires mixed skills, especially as most of the good gear is found in the rock. This is an early season route and should be avoided after winter snows accumulate. There is major avalanche terrain both below and above the route.

Approach Not super obvious from the highway, *Trans-Canada Iceway* can be seen in the eighth main gully from Canmore. It can be identified as a thin white line directly above the park boundary cut line, below a black trian-gular cliff that sits on the ridge. From the Canmore Nordic Centre, bike to the park boundary cut line. There are actually two cut lines so use the first one, the easternmost. Hike up the cut line, traverse into the bowl below the route and slog up to the gully. 4 hours in good conditions. Scramble up snow with little ice steps in the initial 100 m gully to the start of the real climbing.

Gear Standard mixed rack.

1) M5 R, 60 m. Thin and/or snowy ice, that is mainly laidback with some steeper sections. A bolt and pin belay is on the left at the bottom of a small snow field.

2) M5 R, 55 m. Another long pitch with a few little pillars to hook up. A two bolt belay is located on the left below a steep section.

3) WI4, 60 m. A first steep section leads to a snow slope, then a wall of "sandwich" ice. Belay on ice.

Descent Rappel the route. Double 60 m ropes required for the three rappels. The initial 100 m gully can also be rappelled by an anchor (single nut) on the left wall.

West end (near Banff)

Approach Drive through Banff following signs for the Banff Springs Golf Course. Park at the Bow Falls viewpoint behind the Banff Springs Hotel, then walk or bike along the golf course road for about 3 km to a fork. You used to be able to drive your car to this point but the road was closed in the winter of '99/00. Take the right-hand road and follow it for another 1.5 km to where a hiking

Trans-Canada Iceway. *Photo Will Gadd.*

Photo Dave Thomson.

Mount Rundle from the Trans-Canada Highway. A. Two Piece Yanks, B. Sam Goes Trekking, C. Ten Years After, D. Professor Falls Gully, E. Terminator Wall, F. Welcome to Canada Gully, G. The Gulag.

trail branches right (national park interpretive sign with map). Follow the trail through the forest and along the river to where you branch off for your route of choice. More detailed approach information is included with individual route descriptions.

Razor Blade IV M5 WI4 R, 125 m

A thin line of ice that occasionally forms to the left of *Sacre Bleu* on the same cliff band.

Approach Follow the trail past the popular Professor Falls (III WI4, 280 m) to the next drainage. Hike up the right side of the gully, then traverse into the gully itself and climb snow and easy ice steps until below *Sacre Bleu* (IV WI5+, 100 m). Traverse left to the base of *Razor Blade*.

Gear Standard mixed rack.

Make mixed moves up a very short rock section to reach the broken pillar and ice runnel that is followed to its end. Climb in two or three pitches belaying whenever the ice is thick enough.

Descent Rappel route.

Ten Years After IV 5.9 WI5+, 145 m

A sweet line that formed in the winter of 1996/97 and never again.

Approach This is the same approach as for the Terminator Wall. Leave the riverside trail about five minutes before the *Welcome to Canada Gully* (look for flagging tape and/or a bit of a trail branching off). Go up through the forest trending left then angle back right through a short rock band, and back left again to emerge in the *Welcome to Canada Gully*. Cross the gully and go up through the forest on the left to a clearing below a large rock buttress. Continue up and left around the buttress through some small rock steps to the base of the route. Scramble up ledges on the right to a big ledge and belay from rock gear. 2 hours.

Gear Standard mixed rack.

1) 5.9 WI5+ R, 50 m. From the belay ledge, traverse left to a bolt, then keep moving up and left with scant protection to eventually gain an awkward groove/chimney. Climb this feature finding excellent gear in it before swinging around left onto the ice. Follow the narrow ribbon to a sheltered belay ledge on the right consisting of fixed pins and a bomber 2" cam. A direct start (M5+) climbs the lower ice smear, then dry tools straight up 6 m of rock to reach the drip.

Joyti Venne on pitch 1 (direct start) of Ten Years After. *Photo Geoff Trump.*

2) WI5, 45 m. A long sustained pitch of funky, thin ice. Belay at fixed pins on the right wall.

3) M4, 50 m. A final pitch can be climbed up "bathtub smooth chutes" and thin ice past a couple of chockstones.

Descent Either rappel the route from the top of pitch 2 or continue to the top via pitch 3, then exit right onto the ridge. Descend slopes in the direction of the Terminator Wall making one single rope rappel from trees to reach the snow slopes of the Terminator Wall approach.

Two Piece Yanks V 5.11 WI7 (M6+), 225 m

A big route high on Mount Rundle that seems to form frequently. On the first ascent, the leader took a huge fall from the third pitch but came back the next

Ten Years After. *Photo Joyti Venne.*

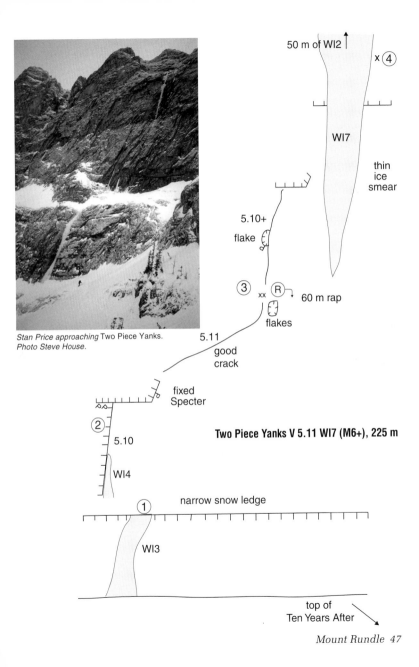

50 m of WI2 ↑

x ④

WI7

thin
ice
smear

5.10+

flake

③ xx ⑧ → 60 m rap

flakes

5.11
good
crack

Stan Price approaching Two Piece Yanks.
Photo Steve House.

fixed
Specter

② 5.10

WI4

Two Piece Yanks V 5.11 WI7 (M6+), 225 m

narrow snow ledge

①

WI3

top of
Ten Years After ↘

day and set the pitch after managing to find good gear. They gave it the sandbag grade M6 saying, "Let them choke on that!"

Approach Either climb *Tens Years After* or turn the rock band on the right via a hidden snow gully. This allows access to the big snow ledge above *Ten Years After*. Traverse this past *Sam Goes Trekking* (WI4) to the base of the route. 3-4 hours.

Gear Standard mixed rack.

1) WI3, 40 m. Easy ice reaches a narrow snow band. Belay from screws.

2) 5.10 WI4, 30 m. Move 10 m left to a right-facing corner containing thin ice and mossy mixed climbing with pitons as the main source of protection. Belay from pitons under a roof.

3) 5.11, 55 m. A long pitch on good quality rock. Climb out right under the roof past a fixed Specter and into a right-trending crack to a bolt and fixed nut anchor at a small stance. Hard dry tooling with thin feet on smooth limestone.

4) 5.10+ WI7, 50 m. Take the crack system above the belay past a flake (fixed pin) and small roof until the ice is thick enough to get on. Very thin and technically challenging ice ends at a single bolt anchor on the right where the steep wall eases off.

5) WI2, 50 m. The final easy ice was climbed on the first ascent to see if the route kept going. It doesn't.

Descent Rappel the route. Two 60 m double ropes from the bolt anchors will reach the bottom.

Jeff Everett on the first ascent of T2.
Photo Serge Angelucci.

The Terminator Wall

This highly visible and imposing wall, also known as the "Trophy Wall," hosts four multi-pitch, traditional mixed routes.

Approach Same as for *Ten Years After*, but from where you branch left for that route, move up and right instead through small trees (usually deep snow) to a rib. Go up the rib, then traverse down and right past a couple of small lee-loaded slopes to a sheltered rock alcove. A short rock band (there is often a bit of fixed rope here) puts you on the snow slope below the WI3 approach pitch to the Terminator Wall proper. 2.5 hours.

Bruce Hendricks battling the crux of Troubled Dreams *(pitch 2). Photo Hendricks collection.*

The imposing Terminator Wall. Photo Dave Thomson.

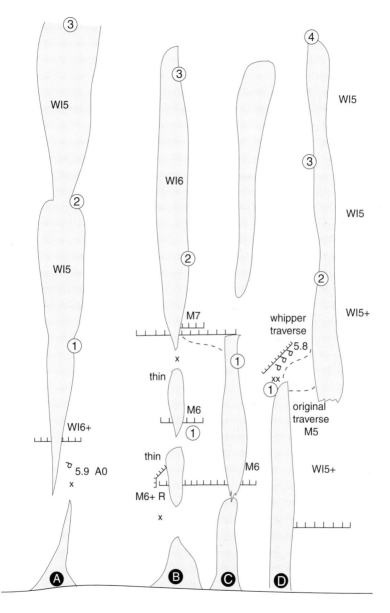

A T2 V 5.9 A0 WI6+, 150 m

The unformed variant of *The Terminator*. Its first ascent involved three people yo-yoing to a high point then returning to jumar their rope and complete the ice. Would go free at about M6 or M7.

Gear Standard mixed rack.

Climb the lower smear of ice to where it thins out and ends. Clip a bolt and stem wide to the hanging dagger. Very steep ice with roofs lead to a cave belay on the right. If the ice doesn't hang far enough down then dry tool the rock to reach it. Two more pitches of aesthetic pillars polish off the difficulties.

Descent Rappel the route.

B Stuck in the Middle V M7 WI6, 145 m

Stuck in the Middle is the unformed, mixed version of *The Replicant* and shares the same crux (M7) of *Troubled Dreams*. The line climbs over three roofs to gain the upper ice.

Gear Standard mixed rack with a few extra pitons.

1) M6+ R, 30 m. Climb very thin ice to gain a crack/weakness on the left side of the ice smear. Follow this crack (one bolt), passing the roof on the left side. The crack becomes a corner that arcs to the right and eventually allows passage to fat ice (possible belay), which gets thinner as it leads to the second roof (belay using TCUs and pins).

2) M7, 55 m. Pull over the roof (M6+) and climb diminishing ice. Continue up thin ice and a loose, vertical rock section (one bolt) to the base of the third and final roof. This is where *Troubled Dreams* traverses in from the right.

Pull out over the roof (M7) and climb steep ice to the end of the rope. Belay off of screws.

3) WI6, 60 m. Steep ice to the top.

Descent Rappel using Abalakovs.

C Troubled Dreams V M7 WI6, 145 m

At the time, *Troubled Dreams* was a cutting edge route that was freed on its second ascent with minimal gear by Alex Lowe. An impressive feat that received a place in *Climbing* magazine's "10 Great Achievements of 1996".

Gear Standard mixed rack.

Between *Postscriptum* (the first pitch of *Sea of Vapors*) and *Stuck in the Middle*, a ribbon of ice occasionally streams from the prominent rock overhang 40 m up. Climb the ice past an overhang at mid-height to a screw anchor near the top. Traverse left on rock under the roof then pull onto thin ice above (M7). This is the same crux as for *Stuck in the Middle*. Continue up a final rope length of steep, sustained ice.

Descent Rappel the route or *Stuck in the Middle*.

D Sea of Vapors V 5.8 WI5+, 165 m

Originally rated WI7+ R, *Sea of Vapors* seems to always form much fatter since its bold first ascent. In regular conditions, it an aesthetic ice climb with an interesting mixed traverse for extra excitement.

Gear Stubbies, screws, pins, TCUs.

1) WI5+, 45 m. Thug up the burly pillar known as *Postscriptum* to a two bolt belay on the left.

2) 5.8 WI5+, 50 m. Directly above the belay climb the right-facing, right-leaning corner (fixed pins) for a few metres to an obvious traverse line right leading to the ice. This is know as the "Whipper Traverse" and is the most common variation. The original line traverses slightly below the belay on thin ice. The difficulty and distance of this traverse depends on the fatness of the ice but is usually around M5 with bad gear.

3-4) WI5, 70 m. A narrow sheet of thick ice to the top.

Descent Rappel the route from Abalakovs and the two bolt anchor on top of pitch 1.

The Gulag

This area is named after the Siberian prison camps and refers to the hard approach and the amount of work it took to complete these routes. A high concentration of some of the technically hardest mixed pitches in the Rockies, if not North America. Located half way up the Welcome to Canada Gully, this deep cave eventually fills in with avalanche debris as the season progresses.

Approach Same as for *Ten Years After* and the Terminator Wall, but at the clearing below the large rock buttress on the left side of the Welcome to Canada Gully, traverse some 200 m right into the gully and up to the cave. Watch out for lee-loaded pockets. 1.5 hours.

Animal Farm M9+/M10-, 25 m

This is one of the technically hardest mixed pitches in North America. Start at a protruding stud (bolt/no hanger) in back of the cave and dry tool near horizontal rock directly toward the ice past 10 bolts. Another line of bolts branches left from the middle of *Animal Farm* and is a project.

Svoboda M9, 25 m

A line of nine bolts up a 45 degree wall to reach the same ice goatee. The first ascent was made without a rope because avalanche debris nearly filled in the cave making it an extended boulder problem.

Ben Firth pushing the limits on Animal Farm. Photo Darcy Chilton.

Rob Orvig and James Blench and Larry Stanier on pitch 2 of Shampoo Planet. The "moss traverse" is a couple of metres directly above the leader.

Photo Joe Josephson.

Shampoo Planet III 5.9 WI3 R (M5), 190 m

A classic traditional mixed route that is best done early in the season before the thin ice on it melts away.

Approach The route will be visible on the lower cliff band above the golf course road about 1/2 km before the hiking trail branches off to the right. Hike up open slopes and past some smooth slabs to the base of the route. 1 hour.

Gear Standard mixed rack.

1) M5, 40 m. Climb a short, thin smear of ice until it ends below an overlap. Move right into a right-facing corner that contains a perfect dry tooling crack (many fixed pins). This is followed to a small stance with a two bolt anchor.

2) M4, 50 m. From the belay, step up and left into a rock groove that is climbed for 5 m to a horizontal moss seam. Traverse left along the moss to thin ice.

3-4) WI3, 100 m. Fun narrow ice climbing leads to the top.

Descent Walk off to the right of *Christmas Present* (the WI3 route to the right), weaving through small cliff bands.

Conditioner Corner III 5.9 R WI3 R, 180 m

Located 10 m left of *Shampoo Planet* is a corner system that offers an alternative start to *Shampoo Planet*.

Approach Same as *Shampoo Planet*.

Gear Pitons (KBs and LAs), TCUs and cams to 2", screws including stubbies.

1) 5.6, 25 m. Pull around a small roof and follow a right-trending corner into a groove. A belay can be construed out of two KBs in the sickle-shaped groove, 1 m below a large ledge. Do not belay at the ledge because the pitch 2 is easier to start from here.

2) 5.9 R WI3 R, 50 m. Follow a shallow groove through a featureless slab to a ledge on the right (5.9 R) just left of the ice. Locate a fixed pin in the corner up and left of the ledge and back it up with a good cam. Traverse out on very thin ice, then climb up 5 m at which point a larger cam can be placed on the left. This is where *Shampoo Planet* joins the ice from the other side.

Descent Same as *Shampoo Planet*.

Sean Isaac on the second ascent of Egypt.
Photo Dave Thomson.

The obscure and rarely formed ice route *Hammer Horror* (WI4+, 30 m), sports a bolted mixed line on either side making it an easy half day outing from Banff or Canmore.

Approach From the Banff east exit, drive north to Lake Minnewanka. Park along the road at the south end of the dam. Hike for 2 km (20 minutes) across the lake to a small outwash fan below the gully. Hike up through trees on the right-hand side of the gully to avoid a rock band, then traverse back into the gully below the climbs. 40 minutes total. Routes are described from left to right. There could be avalanche hazard during times of high snowfall but usually this area is blown dry.

A Egypt M7+, 20 m

Big reaches straight past five bolts directly under the drip. It may be tempting to use the corner out right but the rock is very chossy and is best left untouched.

B Cloud Busting M6+, 20 m

Dry tools rock to the right of the ice before stemming onto it near the top (eight bolts).

Descent Rappel from the two bolt anchor at the top on the left wall.

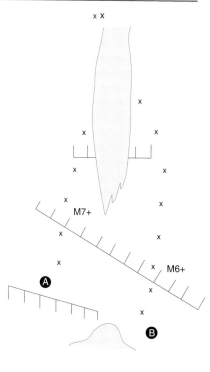

TRANS-CANADA and HIGHWAY 1A
(between Banff and Lake Louise)

The following two routes are within a few metres of each other in the middle of a small cliff above the Trans-Canada Highway near Highway 1A turnoff 4.5 km west of Banff.

Approach Turn off the Trans-Canada Highway onto Highway 1A 5.5 km west of Banff and park at the Fireside Road 400 m from the highway. Follow the road to the trailhead and continue until below the route. Hike straight up through the trees to the climbs. 1 hour. There is no real avalanche danger here as snow on the slope below the routes is usually minimal.

Rock On and Off II 5.8 WI3, 50 m
Gear Standard mixed rack.

Climb the lower ice and move right to a chimney. Follow this with good protection to a treed ledge and another 15 m of easy ice to the top.

Descent Rappel the route.

The Gunfighter II 5.10+ WI3 R, 50 m
The Gunfighter starts immediately left of *Rock On and Off*. Climb 10 m of ice to a ledge (piton). Traverse right to a bulge and climb it into a gully to a thin smear of ice and a two bolt anchor on the top, left side. A total of six bolts protect the rock portion.

Descent One 50 m double rope rappel reaches the ground from the bolt anchor.

Rock On and Off. *Photo Glen Reisenhofer.*

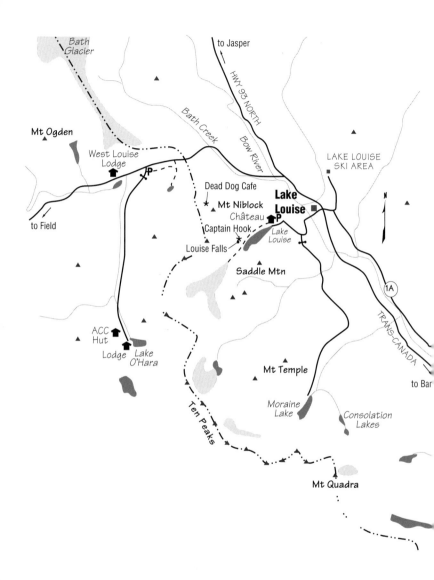

Dog Fight *behind the unformed* Sky Pilot. *Photo Dave Thomson.*

Pilot Mountain

Dog Fight IV M7 WI6+ X, 50 m

Dog Fight is the direct mixed start to the (usually) unformed curtain of *Sky Pilot* (WI6+). The large hanging curtain is easily visible from the Trans-Canada Highway just before Castle Junction when driving west on Pilot Mountain.

Approach Park at the Red Earth Creek trailhead, 11 km past the Sunshine Village turnoff. Follow the popular ski trail for 1.5 km until the trees thin on the left, then head southeast through the woods to a gully that leads to the climb. 2.5 hours. There are major avalanche slopes below and above this route.

Dry tool 15 m of rock past nine bolts to a free-hanging drip. Peck gently up it for 10 m to where it bonds to the rock overhang, then continue more easily to the top. The "X" in the grade is for the huge ride one would take if the dagger broke. The route may be easier or harder depending on how far down the drip hangs.

Descent Rappel with double ropes.

Storm Mountain

Two prominent left-facing corner systems are found on the north side of the lower east ridge of Storm Mountain. Both lines offer interesting mixed ice and snow climbing with an alpine character.

Approach From Castle Junction, ski up the marked trail to the Twin Lakes. Shortly before reaching the lower lake, leave the trail and follow a faint drainage up to the upper lake, toward the obvious northeast face of Storm Mountain. Cross the lake and head up a snow slope to the base of the route. 3 hours.

Gear Standard mixed rack for both routes described below.

Extended Mix V M5 WI4+, 400 m

This is the left-hand of the two mixed gully systems.

The first pitch climbs a ribbon of thin ice up the gully (M5, 50 m). All protection is from the rock. Belay below a short, steep curtain. The second pitch climbs the curtain to below a roof, trends left and finishes up a beautiful narrow stream of thicker ice (WI4+, 50 m). The remainder of the route negotiates small snowfields interspersed with steeper sections (WI3+), and was simul-climbed on the first ascent. At the top of the gully, a number of exits are possible, all involving a short section of mixed ground and/or cornice.

The French Connection M4+ WI4, 400 m

The right corner/gully system was the scene of a bold solo first ascent. As it has not yet been repeated, specific pitch descriptions are unavailable.

Climb a thin pillar (WI4) and continue past a couple of bulges to a 30 cm-wide ribbon of ice. This leads to a snow basin and a bit more ice. Trend left over sketchy, snow-covered slabs to avoid the roofs overhead, then continue left across snow ribs. At the final roof, move back right and break through it via a short, wide crack, then punch through the cornice.

Descent For both routes, walk down the lower east ridge of Storm Mountain to a small saddle at treeline, then down climb a snow gully on the north side of the ridge. No rappels necessary.

Contour back to the Upper Twin Lake and your skis. One hour from the top of the route.

Protection Valley

Protection Valley is between Castle Mountain and Protection Mountain (next mountain to the west) and hosts two difficult-to-access multi-pitch mixed routes. Both of these climbs were originally done as overnight outings.

Approach From Castle Junction, drive north along Highway 1A to where Protection Creek comes out of the valley between Castle and Protection Mountain. Don't go straight up the creek unless the snow is super deep enough to bury the heinous deadfall. Instead, drive back up the hill toward Castle Junction until the hill flattens out and there is a fairly obvious clearing on the north side of the road. Park here. Head through the forest and up toward a rocky outcrop below the west end of Castle. Get on the bench on top of this outcrop by the right side, then head toward the creek contouring and gaining elevation slowly. Eventually, this will deposit you into the creekbed, which offers good skiing to the end of the valley. Go left and climb some steep, treed slopes to reach a hanging valley with a lake. This is definitely avalanche country so heads up. A large boulder offers a decent bivy spot. 4-5 hours.

Superlight V 5.10 WI5+, 230 m

Superlight is located on the big rock wall on the left side of the valley.

Gear Standard mixed rack.

1) 5.5, 30 m. Easy climbing to a nice ledge.

2) 5.10, 50 m. Climb up and left to a large right-facing corner that is followed until you can traverse right to a spacious ledge.

3-5) WI5+, 150 m. A short section of mixed (M6) gains the ice, which weaves up steep mushrooms and pillars to finish on a big ledge.

Descent Approximately 50 m right (northeast) from the top of the route is a buttress with a two bolt rap station. Three more bolt and mixed gear stations reach the ground.

Mon Ami V 5.6 WI4+, 150 m

Located on the right side of the valley, near the back of the cirque. The upper ice can be seen most years from the highway. Sometimes two lines form here. *Mon Ami* is the right-hand one and is usually the thicker of the two (map reference: 82 0/5 717880).

Gear Standard mixed rack.

Traverse a wide snow ledge in from the left to the start of the ice. The first pitch is the crux with a 5.6 chockstone in the gully. Continue up two more pitches of steep pillars.

Descent Rappel the route from Abalakovs, then traverse back across the approach ledge.

Superlight. *Photo Will Gadd.*

Grant Statham on the first ascent of Captain Hook. *Photo Dion Bretzloff.*

Lake Louise

Captain Hook M7+, 20 m

This is the icicle that pours over the huge quartzite roof just right of the first pitch of *Louise Falls*. It doesn't always form, but when it does it is usually in early April and will offer pumpy dry tooling with bomber natural protection. Louise Falls area is free from avalanche danger unless the hazard is extreme.

Approach From the large parking area beside the Chateau Lake Louise follow the wide tourist trail around the right side of Lake Louise to the cliffs on the other end known as "The Back of the Lake." *Louise Falls* will be obvious on your right at the end of the lake where the trail starts to go up hill.

Gear Half set of nuts (mainly small), TCUs to 1", many cams from 2" to 3", screws and stubbies.

Climb the first 15 m of Louise Falls and belay from ice screws on the far right side of a bench. *Captain Hook* traverses right past a fixed pin, then rails across a horizontal crack under a big roof to gain the icicle.

Descent Rappel *Louise Falls* from Abalakovs or trees.

STORM CREEK HEADWALL

A smaller version of the Stanley Headwall, Storm Creek Headwall is one valley east of Stanley and has the same aspect. Enticing smears can be seen from the highway but the two climbs described are out of sight farther up the valley. The potential for new mixed routes is vast. There are huge quantities of dead fall so the approach is best left for later in the season when the snow pack covers these obstacles.

Approach Park on the side of Highway 93, 11.5 km west of Castle Junction overpass. Ski up either side of the drainage through burnt trees avoiding the creek bottom itself. A small cliff is be turned on the right. The routes will be visible on the right starting with *Fleshlumpeater*. 2 hours. There is serious avalanche terrain below and above routes.

Fleshlumpeater IV M6 WI5+, 90 m

This rarely formed line is found shortly after entering the valley about 100 m right of the ice climb *The Shocking Alternative* (IV WI4, 100 m).

1) WI5+ 5.10- (M6), 45 m. Steep, mushroomed ice ends in three bolts of rock climbing to gain a two bolt anchor and semi-hanging stance left of the upper ice dagger.

2) M6 WI5, 45 m. Rock climb right past two bolts to snag the dagger, then pull onto the front of it. There is straightforward ice to the top.

Descent Rappel the route.

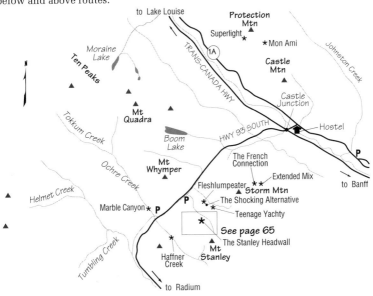

Teenage Yachty IV M5+, 70 m

This route follows thin ice and mixed features on the right margin of the pure ice route *Crash* (WI6). There is a taste of both traditionally protected mixed as well as a bolted dry tooling section.

1) M5-, 45 m. Thin ice leads into a short corner/chimney with a vein of ice in the back, conveniently protected by a cam/nut crack on the right wall. From the top of the corner climb thicker ice to a ledge and two bolt belay.

2) M5+, 25 m. Three bolts protect a short rock wall to reach the ice above. Belay from ice anchors.

Gear Standard mixed rack.

Descent Rappel the route.

Right: Tom Wolfe on the first ascent of Teenage Yachty. Photo Sean Isaac. Below: Fleshlumpeater is on the right and the ice route Shocking Alternative is on the left. Photo Keith Haberl.

The Stanley Headwall is one of the best big mixed venues in the Rockies, if not the world. When the headwall is properly formed, it hosts 11 mixed testpieces. These are all multi-pitch endeavours in a semi-alpine location with numerous hazards. The routes themselves are technically difficult with hard rock and ice. They all contain sections of serious climbing and even the ones that have bolts for protection should not be considered "sport" routes.

Approach Turn west off of the Trans-Canada at Castle Junction and drive 13.5 km along Highway 93 south to the Stanley Glacier parking area and trailhead (sign). A good ski trail switchbacks up forested slopes and delivers you in the valley with Stanley Headwall on your right. Follow the valley bottom until below your desired route, then make your way up exposed, open slopes to its base. One to two hours depending on snow conditions. For the *French Reality* and *The Day After...* area, post hole up the wooded shoulder on the far right side of the headwall to a traverse ledge leading left to the routes. This ledge is subject to much spindrift and wind loading so heads up for snow conditions. The run out off the cliff bands below is uncompromising if caught in an avalanche. A bolt has been placed every 30 to 50 m between *French Toast* and *The Day After...* facilitating a running belay across the ledge system. The entire Stanley Valley is serious avalanche country. The area between *Suffer Machine* and *Nemesis* is threatened by acres of snowy terrain from above while all the routes can be potentially dangerous to approach in the wrong conditions.

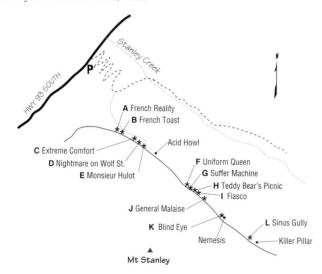

A French Reality V 5.8 WI6+, 150 m

Awesome mixed climbing in a thinly iced corner leads to two very steep pitches of mushroomed pillars.

Gear Standard mix rack.

Sketch up a short mixed step (WI3 when ice) to low-angled terrain. Belay on rock at the base of the next steep section. Pitch 2 moves up thinly iced mixed ground to the base of the corner. If the corner is dry then rock climb it directly (5.8), finding adequate gear in the back of it. If it is iced over then it could be harder unless the ice is really thick. Belay at a bolt anchor below the upper mushroomed pillar. Two pitches of very steep ice polish off the difficulties.

Descent Rappel the route from Abalakovs and fixed rock anchors.

Topher Donahue on pitch 2 of French Reality. *Photo Dave Thomson.*

The right side of the Stanley Headwall. A. French Reality, B. French Toast, C. Extreme Comfort, D. Nightmare on Wolf Street, E. Monsieur Hulot. Photo Dave Thomson.

B French Toast V M7 WI5+ R, 130 m

This is the rarely formed smear that discontinuously streams down immediately left of *French Reality*.

Gear 2" cam, screws including stubbies.

1) M6, 25 m. Climb a rock corner past six bolts to where a thin veneer of ice pours off a roof. Pull onto the ice, then swing and kick carefully to a two bolt anchor in a small rock alcove on the right side of the flow.

2) 5.7 WI5, 50 m. Climb thin ice, then where it ends clip a bolt and rock climb left to a two bolt anchor on a small stance. A midsize cam may be useful just before the anchor.

3) M7, 15 m. Dry tool past three bolts and stem gently to the free-hanging curtain of ice. Swing onto the front where it attaches to the rock overhang above.

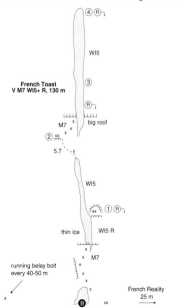

French Toast
V M7 WI5+ R, 130 m

4) WI5, 40 m. A steep narrow pillar ends below a rock roof. Belay on screws.

Descent Rappel the route (see topo).

C Extreme Comfort V 5.11 R A3 WI6+, 180 m

A bold route that wanders across the entire wall from right to left in three very long pitches (all 60 m). It starts at a single bolt anchor to the right of the upper ice (60-80 m right of *Nightmare on Wolf Street*) and finding it may be dependent on the amount of snow built up against the wall. The route finishes on the left of the two upper pillars.

Gear Standard mixed rack including one hook.

1) 5.11, A3, 60 m. Mostly free climbing with the hardest aid move being about two-thirds up the pitch when the leader hung off an A3 hook to put his crampons on for the final mixed section. Just left of the belay bolt climb a short groove and step out left onto a steep wall that is climbed into another longer left-leaning corner. Follow steep ground at the top of the corner onto easier mixed terrain and continue up to a two bolt belay. Aside from the belay bolts there is no other fixed protection.

2) WI 4, 60 m. Climb a short rock groove to a sloping ice ledge (a ledge shared with *Monsieur Hulot*) and traverse to the left edge of the ledge and up rotten ice to a bolt. Traverse rotten ice left to a three bolt belay.

3) WI6, 60 m. Make an exposed traverse left onto the main pillar and climb steep chandeliered ice to the top.

Descent Rappel as for *Nightmare on Wolf Street*.

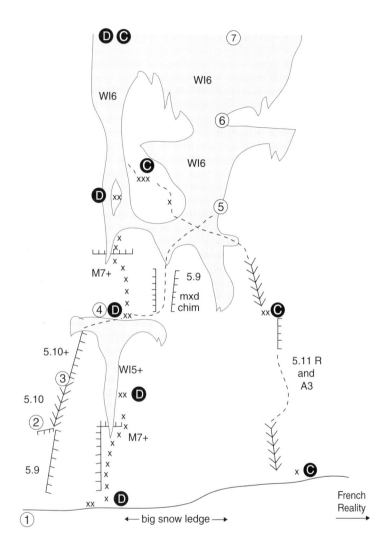

D C

7

WI6

WI6

WI6

C
xxx

D xx

6

5

x

x
x
x
M7+
x
x
x
x
x
x
xx

5.9
mxd
chim

C
xx

5.11 R
and
A3

4 D

5.10+

3

WI5+

xx D

5.10

2

x
x
x
M7+
x
x
x
x
x

5.9

xx x D

1 ← big snow ledge →

x C

French
Reality →

5.8

E

Monsieur Hulot Area

Monsieur Hulot area on the Stanley Headwall. Photo Raphael Slawinski.

D Nightmare on Wolf Street
V M7+ WI6+, 175 m

An awesome line that comes in most years. The first two pitches were climbed in the spring of '97, but the whole route was finally completed in the winter of '99. All the rock sections are well bolted but the ice is hard, serious and usually detached.

Gear Quick draws for nine bolts, screws.

1) M7+, 20 m. The route starts at a two bolt belay below an obvious right-facing corner with the dagger hanging above. Climb a short section of thin face to access the corner and continue past nine bolts in total to gain the ice. A two bolt belay will be found after a few metres behind a skinny freestanding pillar.

2) WI5+, 45 m. Climb the pillar to the prominent ledge where this route crosses *Monsieur Hulot* Two bolt belay.

3) M7+ WI6+, 25 m. Climb an easy, triangle-shaped block of rock to the first bolt. Continue up to the roof and move left to latch onto the hanging ice. There is a total of seven bolts: five before the roof, one at the lip with a sling on it and one 3 m past the lip and slightly left. After 10 m of ice a two bolt belay can be found in an alcove right of the main pillar.

4-5) WI6, 85 m. Continue up very steep ice for two pitches with sheltered belays in caves behind the pillars.

Dave Campbell and Raphael Slawinski on the first pitch of Nightmare on Wolf Street. *Photo Dave Thomson.*

Joe Josephson tackling thin ice on pitch 5 during the first ascent of The Day After les Vacances de Monsieur Hulot. Photo Francois Damilano.

E The Day After les Vacances de Monsieur Hulot V 5.10+ (M7) WI6, 270 m

Originally aided to reach the upper ice, the second ascent freed the rock corners on pitch 3 and 4 to create this challenging natural line. While these pitches are the crux, with little or no ice and traditionally protected dry tooling, the route offers sustained climbing throughout.

Gear Standard mixed rack with double cams in the mid sizes.

1) 5.8, 50 m. The first pitch surmounts a short rock band to gain the large snow ledge that cuts across the bottom of the headwall. Just left of a large rock cave, climb a 10 m rock corner (sometimes ice), then cruise up snow to the base of the headwall proper. This point can also be accessed by traversing in from the right as for the previous four routes.

2) 5.9, 30 m. Climb a shallow, left-facing corner with occasional patches of ice. Belay on a ledge on the left where the corner steepens dramatically (LAs and a large cam useful for belay).

3) 5.10 (M6+), 20 m. Climb the steep corner above, which is awkward at the start, but good cam placements can be found in the cracks on the left wall. Continue more easily to a semi-hanging belay below the next steep section. Belay from small cams and some fixed pins.

4) 5.10+ (M7), 35 m. Continue up the overhanging corner with adequate gear for the hard sections. The rock is very smooth and the feet are bad. Above the corner, move right on easier but run-out and snow-covered rock to the two bolt anchor at the top of pitch 2 of *Nightmare on Wolf Street*.

5) 5.9 (M6), 50 m. Traverse right along the snow ledge into a rock chimney that sometimes hosts a thin vein of ice. Exit the chimney and crawl up and right over scary plate ice to a sheltered belay below the steep, mushroomed ice of the next pitch. Rock gear is useful for belay.

6) WI6, 50 m. Climb steep and technical ice to a comfortable belay in a cave on the left.

7) WI5, 20 m. Steep but good ice leads to an alcove at the top of the climb.

Descent Rappel the route. Take care with stuck ropes rappelling the chimney pitch. The lower part can be descended by rappelling the bottom two pitches of *Nightmare on Wolf Street* from two bolt stations.

Matt Collins freeing pitch 4 during the second ascent of The Day After les Vacances de Monsieur Hulot. *Photo Raphael Slawinski.*

F Uniform Queen V 5.8 M7- WI5, 170 m

A wild natural line of thin ice with the M7 crux conveniently protected by a splitter hand crack that parallels the majority of third pitch.

Gear Standard mixed rack with double cams from 2.5" to 3.5".

1) M4 or 5.8, 40 m. Two starts exist for the first pitch. The original, which climbs a short chimney on the right side of the very thin flow, traverses left of the ice and finally finishes on rock on the left side of the ice. A two bolt station is on a small ledge just left of where the ice curtain is disconnected. The alternate start climbs snowed-up 5.8 rock about 10 m left of the ice to the same ledge.

2) M5 WI5 R, 40 m. From the anchor traverse right to a corner on the other side of the ice, then continue up very thin ice that rears up to 80 degrees in places. A two bolt anchor is under a small roof on the right side of the ice.

3) M7-, 40 m. The ultimate pitch of mixed climbing! A 1" to 2" thick, dead vertical stream of ice border on the right by a perfect crack in immaculate rock. Definitely a rarity in the Rockies. Jam the crack while simultaneously hooking the ice. The crux is where the ice pours over a small roof near the top.

4) WI5, 60 m. Stretch the rope out to finish the last straightforward ice pitch.

Descent Rappel the route from an Abalakov at the top followed by two bolt anchors to the ground.

The prolific Dave Thomson finding perfect hand jams on pitch 3 of Uniform Queen. *Photo Sean Isaac.*

Jeff Everett aid climbing on pitch 1 on the first ascent of Suffer Machine. Photo Glen Reisenhofer.

The Suffer Machine Wall. F. Uniform Queen, *G.* Suffer Machine, *H.* Teddy Bear's Picnic, *I.* Fiasco.
Photo Sean Isaac.

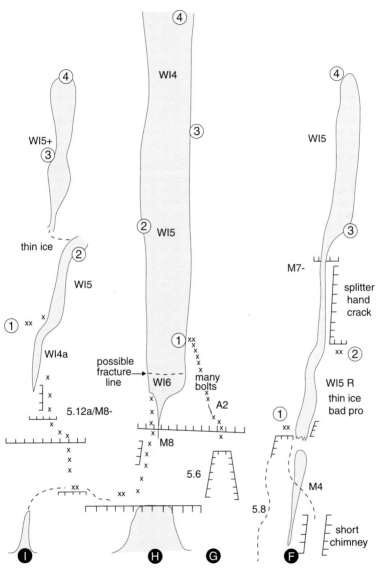

④

WI4

④

④

WI5+
③

WI5

thin ice

②

②

WI5

① xx ˣ

WI4a

ˣ

ˣ
ˣ
ˣ

5.12a/M8-

ˣ ˣ

ˣ
ˣ
ˣ

xx

xx ˣ

③

WI4

④

WI5

M7-

splitter
hand
crack

xx ②

WI5 R

thin ice
bad pro

③

② WI5

①

possible
fracture
line

WI6

ˣ
ˣ
ˣ
ˣ

ˣ

M8

ˣ
ˣ
ˣ
ˣ

5.6

①

xx ˣ

xx ˣ ˣ
ˣ
ˣ
ˣ
ˣ ˣ
ˣ
ˣ

many
bolts

A2

① xx

M4

5.8

short
chimney

Ⓘ Ⓗ Ⓖ Ⓕ

Suffer Machine Wall

G Suffer Machine V 5.6 A1 WI5, 200 m

The first attempt ended when an extension ladder would not reach the ice. Undaunted, the suitors returned and aided the rock to the right, primarily on bolts, then tensioned to the ice. In 1996/97, it formed completely for the first time as a slender WI6+ pillar.

Gear Standard mixed rack plus etriers and ascenders for the aid.

1) 5.6 A1, 50 m. The route begins at the base of an obvious pillar of rock on the right side of the cave. Climb up the right side of the rock pillar to below the roof, then aid past many bolts and the occasional gear place- ment to a two bolt an- chor near the ice.

2) WI5, 50 m. Tension to the ice and climb to a big ledge below the upper half of the route.

3-4) WI4, 100 m. This is straightforward ice in a beautiful position with stun- ning exposure.

Descent Rappel the route.

Jeff Everett experimenting with alternative techniques on an early attempt at Suffer Machine. *Photo Glen Reisenhofer.*

H Teddy Bear's Picnic V M8 WI6, 200 m

The direct start to the unformed drip of *Suffer Machine* producing a free dry tooling variation. During the second ascent, Raphael Slawinski onsighted the rock, but broke the hanging dagger sending him for a 30 m whipper that he miraculously walked away from. The first ascensionists have since added two more bolts, hence making it safer.

Scramble up the initial ice blob and belay at a two bolt anchor on the left.

1) M8 WI6, 40 m. Dry tool chossy yellow limestone, then launch up the huge free-hanging icicle of *Suffer Machine*. Nine bolts protect the rock and the detached dagger. Belay on ice where the angle eases.

2-4) WI4 and 5, 150 m. Follow the ice of *Suffer Machine* to the top.

Descent Rappel the route.

I Fiasco V M8-/5.12a WI5+, 170 m

Twenty metres of overhanging rock leads three pitches of aesthetic ice climbing.

Climb directly up 15 m of thin ice and easy rock to a two bolt belay at the base of pitch 1. Alternatively, climb up and across left from the bolt belay at the base of *Teddy Bear's Picnic*.

1) M8-, 35 m. Nine bolts protect the devious rock moves that can be climbed either barehanded at 5.12a or dry tooled at M8-.

2) WI5, 50 m. A narrow vein eases off into a snow gully that cuts across from *Suffer Machine*. Belay on ice midway up the gully.

3-4) WI5+, 70 m. A thin ice traverse left gains two pitches of steep pillar climbing.

Descent Rappel the route from Abalakovs and bolt anchors.

J General Malaise IV M6 WI5, 90 m

An interesting line that forms 30 m to the left of *Suffer Machine*. Its ice pours from a cave half way up the face.

Gear Standard mixed rack.

1) M3, 20 m. Climb a short rock step in a gully, then plow up snow to a two bolt belay just left of a tiny cave.

2) M6, 40 m. Climbs vertical to less than vertical rock past four widely spaced bolts (some natural gear opportunities in between) to an ice ramp and two bolt anchor on a snow ledge left of the upper pillar. The crux is well protected past the first two bolts while the upper section is easier yet more engaging.

3) WI5, 30 m. Steep ice leads to a narrow cave from which it flows.

Descent Rappel the route from Abalakovs and bolt anchors.

Brian Webster scratching up the crux (pitch 2) of General Malaise. Photo Jim Gudjonson.

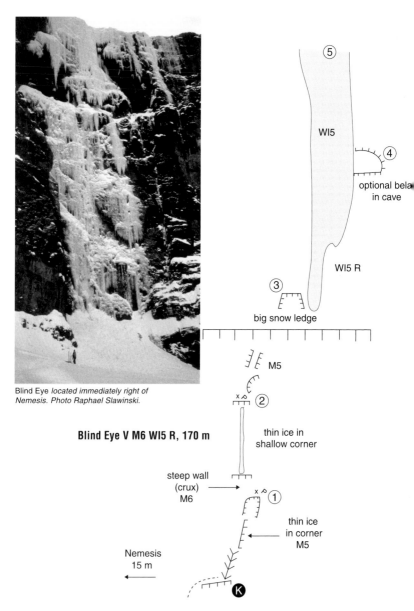

Blind Eye *located immediately right of Nemesis. Photo Raphael Slawinski.*

⑤

WI5

④

optional bela
in cave

WI5 R

③ big snow ledge

M5

② thin ice in
shallow corner

steep wall
(crux)
M6

thin ice in
shallow corner

① thin ice
in corner
M5

Blind Eye V M6 WI5 R, 170 m

Nemesis
15 m

Ⓚ

K Blind Eye V M6 WI5 R, 170 m

This fully mixed route starts 15 m right of *Nemesis*, and follows a system of thinly iced shallow corners to the halfway ledge. It finishes up a steep ice flow 25 m right of *Nemesis*.

Gear Standard mixed rack with a few more cams and pins.

1) M5, 30 m. Follows a steepening gully to a small belay on top of a pinnacle on the right (bolt and pin belay).

2) M6, 30 m. Climbs thin ice on the steep wall above to another hanging belay (bolt and fixed Specter) at the base of the exit chimney.

3) M5, 50 m. Climbs the chimney (poorly protected near the top) to thin ice and eventually the snow ledge halfway up *Nemesis*. Trend right over a rock step to the base of the upper flow.

4-5) WI5 R, 60 m. Gain the main flow over some thin and detached ice (poorly protected to start). Climb in one long pitch or two 30 m pitches with a sheltered cave belay on the right.

Descent Rappel the route or rappel *Nemesis*.

L Sinus Gully IV 5.6 WI3, 75 m

A short route with a big approach, *Sinus Gully* is the easiest mixed route on the Stanley Headwall.

Gear Standard mixed rack.

Climb a long pitch of undulating ice (WI3) to an ice belay in a cave below rock overhangs. Begin the next pitch by climbing rock (5.6) to a traverse line that widens into a ledge. Follow this left for a rope length to a short step of ice that exits onto the snow slopes.

Descent Slog left (beware of avalanche potential) and either rappel from an Abalakov at the top of *Killer Pillar* (the next ice route to the left) with double 60 m ropes or keep walking left until the cliff ends and you can return to the base of the climb.

Raphael Slawinski and Chris Geisler on the first ascent of Blind Eye. *Photo Matt Collins.*

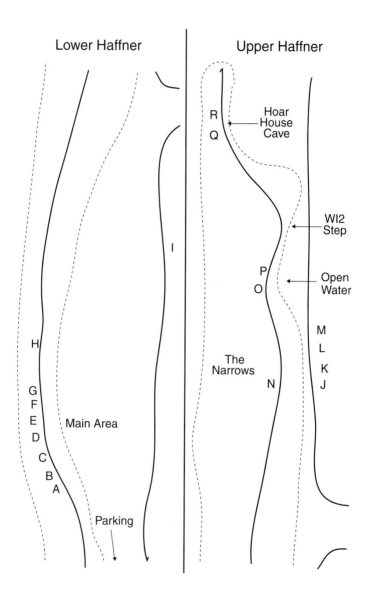

Lower Haffner

Upper Haffner

Hoar
House
Cave

WI2
Step

Open
Water

The
Narrows

Main Area

Parking

R
Q

P
O

N

M
L
K
J

I

H
G
F
E
D
C
B
A

Mixed climbing originated in the big mountains but has found its way down to the crags and canyons with Haffner Creek leading the way. This narrow canyon is THE mixed crag of the Canadian Rockies, hosting 18 pick-dulling routes ranging from well-protected moderates to one of the hardest mixed pitches in North America.

In a way, Haffner is responsible for the rapid rise of standards in the Rockies. Novice mixed climbers can find safe, bolted M5s and M6s to test their on-sight abilities on, or whip off of, without the repercussion of more serious routes. With zero avalanche hazard, Haffner is ideal for when snow conditions are dangerous or a low commitment day is in order.

Approach Park at the Marble Canyon parking lot 17.5 km from the Castle Junction turn off on the Trans-Canada. Cross the highway and follow a well-packed trail through the parks campground and into the canyon. 20 minutes. Routes are described as you walk upstream. Refer to map and topos for exact locations.

A The Boyd Mystery M8, 20 m

Powerful moves on very small edges crank out double roofs (five bolts) before stepping onto the ice.

B Half 'n' Half M6+, 20 m

This classic was the first bolted line in Haffner Creek. It's M7 in lean years when the ice does not hang down over the roof. Good holds and solid rock on a blunt arete lead to a 45 degree overhang and the ice (four bolts).

C Mojo M8+, 20 m

Constantly changing owing to breaking holds, *Mojo* pulls a series of small roofs and a thin smear of ice before swinging onto the hanging icicle right of *Half 'n' Half* (six bolts).

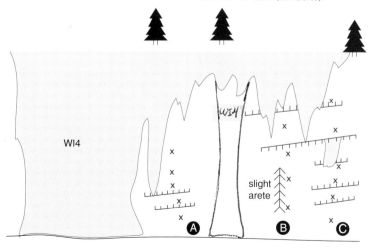

Grant Meekins on the burly Swank. *Photo Sean Isaac.*

D Shagadelic M7, 15 m

A balancey slab to technical torquing in a short crack (five bolts).

E Half a Gronk M5+, 15 m

Three bolts up a left-leaning corner to the ice.

F The Flake Route M5, 15 m

Jam up the right side of the conspicuous flake, then step left onto the ice clipping a bolt on the way. The flake will accept 2" to 3" cams, or better yet, lasso the top of it with a double length sling.

G Swank M8-, 15 m

Bouldery moves burl out a big roof leading to a verglassed corner. Six bolts (no screws needed) and a two bolt anchor on a ledge below the top of the cliff.

H Minimal Impact M5+, 20 m

Originally lead on gear (or lack of!), this ephemeral smear was retrobolted (two bolts) by two climbers unaware of its bold first ascent.

Simon Parsons on Mojo. Photo Roger Chayer.

big ledge

WI4+

WI4

WI3

D E F G

The next route is found by itself in a deep cave on the opposite side of the canyon.

I In Reverse M7, 15 m

Short but steep! Power out the cave to hook a meager smear of yellow ice (four bolts). Formed in the winter of '99/00 but may never be there again as it was probably a fluke ground seep.

Sean Isaac on the first ascent of In Reverse. *Photo Darcy Chilton.*

Guy Lacelle going for the ice on The River Runs Through It. *Photo Sean Isaac.*

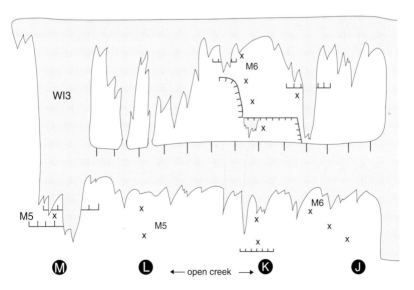

Sean Isaac on his horizontal testpiece, Caveman, in the Hoar House Cave. Photo Roger Chayer.

The next four routes are on the right side of the "Narrows" just before the waterfall and pool.

J The River Runs Through It M6, 25 m

Make a rising traverse left past three bolts to the ice, then scramble up onto a ledge behind the upper pillar. Clip one last bolt on the left side before jumping on the dagger (four bolts total).

K Nasty Infection M6, 25 m

Two bolts worth of dry tooling gain the ice ledge. Clip a bolt from the ledge and make a slippery mantle past a thin smear and into a right-facing corner/flake. This is climbed past three more bolts to steep moves onto the final, short bit of ice. Six bolts in total.

L Surfin' Safari M5, 25 m

Dry tool past two bolts, then continue up a series of steep, lacy pillars.

M Splashdown M5, 25 m

One bolt protects a short section of rock moves before romping up the WI3 flow above. A great introductory route.

These three routes are located on the opposite wall of the narrow canyon to the previous four.

N Put on Your Huggies M5+, 20 m

Dribbles of ice occasionally glaze the deep corner/chimney directly across from *The River Runs Through It*. A hard lead with challenging gear.

Gear Standard mixed rack.

O The Gong Show M8+/M9-, 10 m

A technical slab leads to hard pulls out a roof, then muckle over the lip onto the ledge (five bolts). A second pitch still awaits a first ascent.

P Don't Mess With Da Nest M7, 10 m

Climb a skinny pillar, then plug a bunch of gear in a horizontal crack before firing the final moves out the roof to the ice. Be careful on the bird's nest.

Gear Standard mixed rack.

The following two climbs are located in Upper Haffner Creek in a huge cave dubbed the Hoar House after the fist-sized hoar frost crystals caked on its roof. Access is by either scrambling up the short waterfall at the end of the canyon (if frozen) or by rappelling in from above. To gain the top, hike up through the trees on the left side just before entering the lower canyon. Follow the rim until above the Hoar House, then rappel in from a tree on the edge. Alternatively, keep hiking for another 100 m to where the canyon cliffs end then descend on foot and walk back downstream to the cave.

Q Dick Jones M7-, 15 m

A warm-up for the business to the right. Steep moves out a roof and into a chossy corner gain a small tongue of ice. Continue up thin ice and moss to a tree anchor (five bolts).

R Caveman M9+, 15 m

Ridiculously steep! This is one of the technically hardest mixed pitches in North America. Ten metres of horizontal dry tooling and verglassed holds lead to a dead tree decorated with ice (11 bolts and two bolt anchor). Don't blow the first few clips or you will land on your head.

MARBLE CANYON

This is one of the first sport mixed areas to be developed in the Rockies. Unfortunately, it forms differently most seasons; however, the three routes described below are excellent and can usually be climbed. No avalanche hazard.

Approach Park at the Marble Canyon parking lot located on the north side of Highway 93, 17.5 km west of the Castle Junction turn off. Follow the Marble Canyon nature trail to the fifth bridge. 10 minutes. See map for location of routes.

A Fantasy Shower M7+, 30 m

Fantasy Shower is everything that *Reality Bath* isn't: short, safe and fun. Rappel into the route from a tree just before the fifth bridge. The rock is quite steep so clip bolts on the way down in order to reach the belay. This route climbs rock (five bolts) on the opposite side of the narrow gorge, then swings onto ice topping out on the other side. Belay at a one bolt anchor on small stance 2 m above the creek. This stance can also be reached by walking along the creek ice and scrambling up to it from the right.

B Swine Dive M7, 30 m

Just right of main ice pillar (*Tokkum Pole* WI5+, 40 m), devious rock moves past three bolts gain the curtain of ice that is followed to a two bolt anchor at the top just below the bridge.

C Throttler M7-, 30 m

Located behind the exit ice flow (*Marble Arch* WI3, 40 m), three bolts worth of dry tooling hit the ice. To access this route, either rappel from trees around the chockstones into the base of it or walk on the frozen ice of the creek from the other routes. Beware that the creek ice can be very thin around here with deep pools below. It is possible to break through into the flowing water below, never to be seen again.

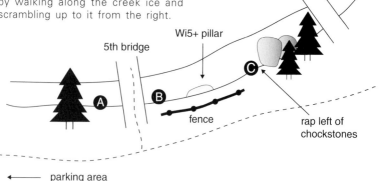

6th bridge

Wi5+ pillar

5th bridge

fence

rap left of
chockstones

← parking area

Hobey Walker on Fantasy Shower. *Photo Dave Thomson.*

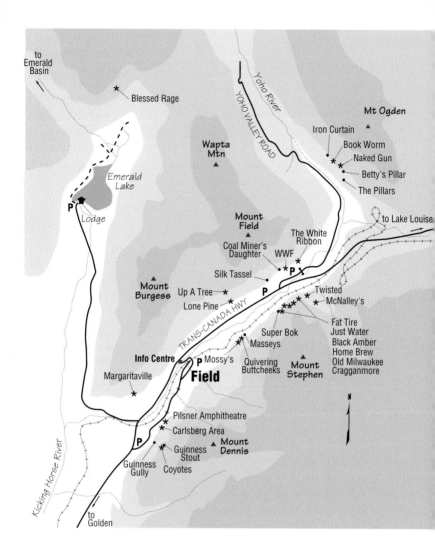

to
Emerald
Basin

* Blessed Rage

Yoho River

YOHO VALLEY ROAD

Mt Ogden ▲

Iron Curtain

Wapta
Mtn ▲

Book Worm
* * Naked Gun
• Betty's Pillar
The Pillars

Emerald
Lake

P
Lodge

to Lake Louise →

Mount
Field ▲

The White
Ribbon
Coal Miner's   WWF
Daughter   • *
Silk Tassel •   P
Mount   * P
Burgess ▲ Up A Tree *   Twisted
Lone Pine *   * *** * McNalley's

TRANS-CANADA HWY

Fat Tire
Just Water
Super Bok   Black Amber
Masseys   Home Brew
Info Centre • P Mossy's Quivering   Old Milwaukee
Margaritaville   Buttcheeks Mount   Cragganmore
*   Field   Stephen ▲

N

P
Pilsner Amphitheatre
* * Carlsberg Area
P   * Mount
* Guinness Dennis ▲
Guinness Stout
Gully   Coyotes

Kicking Horse River

to
Golden

YOHO NATIONAL PARK

Mount Niblock

Dead Dog Cafe IV M6 WI5, 55 m

An excellent route but it is not known if it forms every year. Definitely worth the ski in to check it out, though.

Approach From Lake O'Hara parking 12.7 km west of Lake Louise on the Trans-Canada Highway, ski 3 km east on Highway 1A (closed in winter) to the "The Great Divide" sign. Turn right and follow the drainage for two hours until the drips are visible on your left on the west face of Mount Niblock (map reference: 82 N/8 503961). There is some avalanche hazard on the final section of the approach. Although there is no hazard above the route itself.

1) WI5, 20 m. Climb a short steep pillar and belay off of ice screws in a cave behind the upper 10 m pillar.

2) M6, 35 m. Climb 10 m of WI4 and pull into a 5.9 crack ending at a roof (5.10). Clip a bolt and pull the roof left onto a small patch of ice and a ledge. Climb another shorter section of rock (one bolt) to gain the final ice.

Gear Standard mixed rack.

Descent One rappel with double 55 m or 60 m ropes from Abalakov.

Field is home to countless drips and smears tucked in gullies and obscure cliffs. Some of the routes like *Fat Tire* and *Just Water* may form differently every year or may never form again. Other routes have been claimed then reclaimed a few years later. All of this makes it very confusing to sort out what's what.

Mount Stephen

Approach For all the routes on Mount Stephen, except around Massy's, park at the Takakkaw Falls parking area on the north side of the highway at the bottom of the big hill descending into Field. Cross the highway and follow the crest of the obvious man made "lateral moraine" to the train tracks under the north ridge of Mount Stephen. The following eight routes are all accessed by walking west along the tracks until underneath your climb of desire. *McNalley's* and *Twisted* lie east of the tunnel while the other six are west of the tunnel. All the routes on Mount Stephen have avalanche prone slopes on the approaches and/or in the gullies above. Please do not mess with any of the avalanche detection wiring or trigger gates. These are found just above the tracks to alert Canadian Pacific Railway of avalanche debris.

McNalley's M6, 25 m

A single pitch climb located 60 m left of *Twisted*.

Gear Screws, cams to 2".

Climb a short smear to a roof with a bolt out left. Pull the roof onto thin ice clipping another bolt. A few cam placements lead to the final budge (bolt) and upper ice. There is a total of three bolts on the route.

Descent Rappel from a tree on top.

Twisted III 5.9 WI3 R, 120 m

Twisted is the obvious smear right on the buttress and is clearly visible as you drive by. Slog up a steep snow slope from the tracks to the base of the route in 45 minutes.

Gear Standard mixed rack.

1) WI3, 20 m. Easy ice ends under a steep rock wall.

2) 5.6, 50 m. Move right until low angled mixed ground can be accessed. Climb up and left to a natural gear anchor at the base of the crux rock corner.

3) 5.9 WI3 R, 25 m. Dry tool a right-facing quartzite corner, then step left onto thin ice. Make an ice belay a short way up the gully.

4) WI3, 25 m. Climb a final pillar of good ice.

Descent Rappel the route from Abalakov anchors.

Fat Tire II 5.8 WI4 R, 95 m

A thin ice line found in the gully 150 m right of *Twisted* (map reference: 82 N/8 958388).

Approach Walk through the tunnel and head up the gully to a rock band that is climbed on the left. Traverse snow slopes to the base of the route.

Gear Standard mixed rack.

1) 5.7 WI4 R, 45 m. Climb a 3 m left-facing corner, then go up a narrow vein of thin ice to a screw belay in good ice before the next mixed section.

Brian Webster enjoying solid quartzite on the crux of Twisted *(pitch 3). Photo Sean Isaac.*

2) 5.8 WI4, 40 m. Trend right over thinly ice mixed rock to gain a brief WI4 pillar and screw belay at the base of the final 10 m ice pillar.

3) WI4, 10 m. A final, short pillar reaches the top.

Descent Rappel the route from Abalakovs.

Just Water III 5.10 WI5, 55 m

Located on the lowest cliff band between *Twisted* and *Home Brew*, it forms as a distinct, thin vein of ice below a prominent roof. A narrow avalanche path leads straight up to the base of the route from the railroad tracks.

Gear Standard mixed rack.

Climb thin ice, frozen moss and rock in a big left-facing corner with good gear to a narrow column of ice (belay with screws and gear). A thin and difficult to protect crack leads to a roof with more ice below it. Follow a ledge right on frozen moss with good rock gear to a tree belay.

Descent Double rope 55 m rappel from the trees.

Black Amber M6, 25 m

Black Amber is found on a cliff low in the trees about 300 m left of *Home Brew*. It climbs a mixed left-facing corner past six bolts to a two bolt anchor. This may actually be part of the first pitch of *Just Water*.

Home Brew IV 5.10 WI5, 60 m

Home Brew is the first major gully system encountered when hiking west along the tracks.

The climbing has an "alpine feel" to it (i.e. run out chimney).

Larry Stanier approaching the difficulties on Home Brew. *Photo Grant Statham.*

Climb up to some ice, then move left on a sloping ledge to a right-facing corner. Clip fixed pins then move up and right into the chimney/slot. Run it out until the ice is thick enough for an anchor or stretch the rope out to the top. This route could use a bolted anchor on top.

Gear Standard mixed rack. A 4" or 5" cam may alleviate the long run-out in the chimney.

Descent Rappel from what ever manky anchors you can arrange.

Old Milwaukee III M7, 50 m

This fun route is located on a small quartzite wall between *Home Brew* gully and *Super Bok* gully. It can be seen from the highway low in the trees.

Steve House on pitch 2 of Old Milwaukee.
Photo Brian Cox.

Gear Standard mixed rack with a few extra mid-sized cams for pitch 2.

1) M7-, 25 m. Vertical ice leads to a stance under a roof. Clip some fixed gear and hunt for more before firing the steep moves to the ice.

2) M7, 25 m. The second pitch is usually pure rock (5.10) but can occasionally be iced up, like the first ascent. Pull a small roof then up the crack to a belay (small tree and fixed pin) in an alcove.

Descent Rappel from the anchor (tree and piton) with double ropes.

Cragganmore IV 5.8 WI4, 200 m

Cragganmore climbs thin ice and mixed terrain in the gully left of *Super Bok* (IV WI5, 300 m). It is a broad gully with ice

pouring from steep rock bands separated by short snow bowls. The last pitch misses the big rock roof and hanging dagger by climbing a mixed corner out left.

Approach Follow the tracks west until under the open snow gully that leads up to *Super Bok*. The first pitch begins where *Super Bok* climbs under the natural rock arch.

Gear Standard mixed rack.

1) WI3, 35 m. Climb a short step of ice (may be thin) and belay on ice at the base of a snow gully.

2) 5.8 WI4, 15 m. A short section of rock allows access to the hanging drip. More snow leads to the base of the next pitch.

3) WI3, 40 m. Climb a 20 m WI3 pillar (big free hanging dagger above) then traverse a ledge 20 m left. Build a rock anchor at the base of the corner that begins the next pitch.

4) 5.7 WI4, 60 m. A sweet right-facing corner laced with ice leads to a fatter flow of ice.

Descent Hike right through the trees and rappel *Super Bok* from Abalakovs.

Massy's Waterfall

The first pitch of *Massy's* has two classic traditional mixed routes that form on its right side. They are described from left to right.

Approach Drive into the field and park at a large plowed pull out near the tracks on the east end of town. Follow the tracks east then go up the creekbed to the route. 45 minutes.

Quivering Buttcheeks
III 5.9 WI5 (M5), 30 m

Climb the big corner immediately right of *Massy's* for 10 m to where it ends below a roof, then traverse left to the ice.

Gear KBs, LAs, Angles, screws.

Mossy's 5.10 WI5, 35 m

Either traverse in from the right on a narrow ledge or climb directly up a short icy corner to reach the same point. Clip a bolt and move up into a left-facing corner. From the top of the corner traverse horizontally left to reach the ice.

Gear Standard mixed rack.

Descent For both routes, a single 60 m rope rappel from an Abalakov will reach the ground.

Jim Racette on the direct start to Mossy's.
Photo Sean Isaac.

Mount Dennis

Approach Drive into "downtown" Field and from its west end gain the one-way westbound dirt road that follows the base of Mount Dennis back to the highway. A plowed parking area is on the left (bulletin board) just before rejoining the Trans-Canada Highway. Park here for all mixed routes on Mount Dennis. Walk back down the road to *Pilsner Pillar* and *Carlsberg Column*. Hike up through trees into their respective drainages.

Pilsner Amphitheatre

Last Call M7- WI5, 45 m

Fun bolted mixed climbing behind *Pilsner Pillar* that sometimes ices up completely. Climb rock and small icicles past five bolts to gain the ice of *Pilsner Pillar* at the lip of the cave.

Wart Hog M5 WI6, 45 m
Gear Standard mixed rack.

Clip the first bolt on *Last Call*, then traverse right on natural gear to the unformed ice pillar.

Descent Rappel both routes (double ropes), either from Abalakov at top of ice or rock anchor back and right.

Carlsberg Area

Shooter Bar M7, 30 m

From a two bolt anchor on the right side of *Cascade Kronenbourg* climb the left-facing corner above to an old self-drive bolt. Move out of the corner past two more bolts and onto a ledge. Another three bolts allow access to the upper 5 m of ice and a two bolt chain belay at a stance out right.

Brad Wrobleski stemming delicately onto Wart Hog. *Photo Dave Chase.*

Silent Sam M7, 30 m

Located down and 60 m right of *Cascade Kronenbourg* (WI5+) is a large left-facing corner smeared with thin ice. The start of the route is accessed by walking 20 m right along a snow ledge that starts about 40 m right of *Cascade Kronenbourg*. Belay at a single bolt anchor.

There are a total of eight bolts on the route: four on the lower wall, two in the corner and two above the roof. Belay from a tree on top.

Guinness Gully

Coyotes III 5.9 WI5, 50 m

This route is located to the right of *Guinness Stout* (IV WI4+, 80 m) requiring you to climb *Guinness Gully* (III WI4, 245 m) to access it.

Approach From the plowed parking area, *Guinness Gully* should be visible through the trees almost straight above. Hike steeply (normally well-trodden trail) to the base of *Guinness Gully*. Climb *Guinness Gully* then slog up to the base of *Guinness Stout* (left-hand of two ice routes) and *Coyotes*.

Gear Standard mixed rack.

From the bottom of the upper, steep section of *Guinness Stout*, move right and climb a small curtain of ice to WI5 pillar in a left-facing corner. Belay off of screws on top of ice. Move left on thin ice out under a roof (crux) to a left-facing corner (two bolts and gear) that leads to a mossy top out in the trees.

Descent Rappel from the trees with double ropes.

Mount Ogden (Yoho Valley Road)

Approach Park at the Takakkaw Falls parking area on the north side of the highway at the bottom of the big hill descending into Field. Ski along the Yoho Valley Road and cross the river (hopefully frozen) below your route of choice. Both these routes are fairly safe from avalanche danger but be aware of huge avalanche paths when approaching.

Naked Gun M6 WI5, 25 m

Located 10 m right of the ice route *Lagrimas de Alegria* (WI5+) and 300 m left of *The Pillars* (WI4), *Naked Gun* starts at a two bolt belay on a ledge that is accessed from the left. This route sometimes forms as a complete pillar of ice.

Gear Set of nuts, TCUs to 1", screws.

From the two bolt belay, a few gear placements in a flake leads to three bolts, then some more natural gear before stepping onto the ice. A final bolt can be clipped from the ice. A total of four bolts and a two bolt anchor at the top.

Descent Rappel the route.

Bookworm M7-, 30 m

An obvious open book with a deep fissure/chimney laced with icicles about halfway between *Naked Gun* and *Iron Curtain* (WI6).

Stem, chimney and grunt up the ice-glazed slot past eight bolts (on right-hand wall) to a two bolt anchor. More or less ice, depending on the year, can affect the grade and style of climbing.

Descent Rappel the route with a single 60 m rope.

Mount Field

The White Ribbon III 5.8 R WI4, 280 m

Approach Park at the Takakkaw Falls parking area on the north side of the highway at the bottom of the big hill descending into Field. Walk across the campground picnic area to a snow gully at the base of the southeast ridge of Mount Field. Hike up the gully to where it ends at a much steeper gully with an arete on its left side. 20 minutes.

Gear 3 KBs, 2 LAs, screws.

Climb the loose arete on the left side then cross over to its right side and finish at a tree belay (5.8 R, 30 m). A 200 m snow gully deposits you at a base of a nice waterfall pitch tucked into a right-facing corner (WI4, 50 m).

Descent Rappel the route from Abalakovs and trees.

WWF III M6 WI4+, 100 m

This obvious line is located 20 m to the right of *Coal Miner's Daughter* (WI4, 50 m), approximately 2 km east of Field. Some avalanche hazard on the approach but not much above.

Approach Park at the Takakkaw Falls parking area on the north side of the highway at the bottom of the big hill descending into Field. Hike to the right of the drainage through sparse trees to the base of the route. 45 minutes.

Gear Standard mixed rack.

1) M6, 50 m. Climb 5 m of slab ice then move right into a left-facing corner/flake. Follow this a few metres until below a rock overhang with a hanging dagger. Traverse left on thin ice (crux with good cams) and pull into

Eamonn Walsh freeing the first pitch of WWF. *Photo Rob Owens.*

another left-facing corner system. Climb the corner then traverse back right on choss and dirt to gain solid ice. Belay off thin ice.

2) WI4+, 50 m. Thin WI3 with a dubious 10 m pillar near the top.

Descent Rappel both pitches using Abalokov anchors.

Lone Pine III 5.7 WI5, 55 m

Approach Park along the Trans-Canada Highway 1/2 km west of the Takakkaw Falls turnoff. The route will be visible 300 m above as a narrow pillar dripping over roofs capped by a big tree leaning out over the top. Cross the flats and bushwhack through trees for 10 minutes into the gully below the route. Cruise up the gully past some WI2. 45 minutes.

Gear Standard mixed rack.

Climb thin ice in a left-facing corner that arches left near the top. Belay off of screws on a ledge under a rock overhang after 40 m. Pull the rock overhang onto steep ice. Turn the final roof by traversing left on 5.7 rock until it is possible to climb up to the trees. The original line aided directly out the last roof (A2).

Another "mixed" route called *Up a Tree* (M? WI4+, 70 m) is located farther up the same drainage but is better approached by bushwhacking/slogging around to the left of *Lone Pine* (two hours). It climbs a dead tree to below a rock roof that is pulled directly, gaining a narrow pillar.

Descent Rappel *Lone Pine* with double 60 m ropes from a tree on top.

Mount Burgess

Margaritaville III M7, 70 m

Margaritaville seems to form about every other year. It can be identified as a big curtain pouring from the top of the cliff low on the southwest side of Mount Burgess. If "in," it will be obvious from the climbs on Mount Dennis on the other side of the valley.

Approach Park on the side of the road just after turning off (plowed pullout). The route will be visible from here so get oriented as it cannot be seen for most of the approach. Cross the meadow to an old road. Follow the road west (left) to its intersection with the groomed cross-country ski trail. Hike up the hill and contour left until below the route. Zigzag up the steep hill to the base of the route. 1 hour. Avalanche danger is non-existent, however, the steep hill directly

below the route could pose a threat during times of high snowfall.

1) M5, 40 m. Three bolts supplemented with ice screws protect funky ice and mixed climbing to a two bolt anchor at a small stance on the right.

2) M7, 30 m. A thin bit of ice leads to ever steepening rock (10 bolts) and onto the final ice curtain. Belay on ice. After the first ascent in winter '99/00, the thin apron of ice above the belay meted out making for a long unprotected, runout up a slab to get to the first bolt. The first ascensionist plans to return to add a couple more bolts for when the ice in this section is gone.

Descent Rappel the route from first an Abalakov, then the two bolt anchor on top of pitch 1.

Margaritaville. *Photo Jim Gudjonson.*

Emerald Lake

Blessed Rage V 5.7 WI6, 230 m

The first ascent was a bold solo undertaking. Since then it has been repeated as a pure, albeit thin, ice route in fatter ice years.

Approach 1.6 km west of the turnoff into Field turn right onto the Emerald Lake Road and follow it 8 km to the lake and parking area. The route will be visible on the cliffs at the far end of the lake just right of the Emerald Basin drainage. Take the set ski trail around the north side of the lake, then bushwhack steeply through trees to the large snow slope below the route. There are big avalanche slopes both below and above this route. 3 hours.

Gear Standard mixed rack.

A full rope length of WI3 ends in a snow gully. From the top of the gully, mix climb a right-facing corner (5.7) and move left across snowed-up slabs to a fixed belay. Climb scary plate ice to a fixed anchor on the right side of the upper curtain. A single bolt anchor may also be found on the left side of the curtain from the first ascent. The final pitch tackles sustained but good ice (WI6, 55 m).

Descent Rappel the route from Abalakovs and rock anchors.

Blessed Rage.
Photo Grant Statham.

GOLDEN AREA

Yoho Park Gate

Jacob's Ladder IV M7+ WI5, 200 m

Jacob's Ladder is a long mixed route with sunny exposure. Joe Josephson's *Waterfall Ice* guidebook describes the—at-that-time unclimbed—curtain as "an exciting exercise in classic Rockies frigging around involving loose rock and aid climbing." Indeed, the first ascent was classic Rockies frigging around, but in modern terms meaning drilling and cleaning.

Approach Drive the Trans-Canada Highway 1.8 km west of the Yoho Park gate. Park at the plowed pullout on the south side. Walk 200 m east along the highway to a small obvious gully on the north side. Follow this to the climb's base. 1 to 1.5 hours depending on snow conditions. There is a large avalanche gully threatening this climb. Also, pitch 2 is in the line of fire from large hanging daggers, best left alone on warm, sunny days.

1) WI5, 20 m. Climb a pumpy, hollow tube of ice to a bolted belay on the left side.

    Slog up the 200 m snow gully and climb a 5 m WI2 step to reach the base of pitch 2. Belay on the left.

2) WI3, 60 m. Climb a broad shield and some technical mushrooms to reach a bolt belay at the beginning of the rock section.

3) M7+, 25 m. An overhanging and strenuous pure rock pitch with 12 bolts finishing at a two bolt anchor.

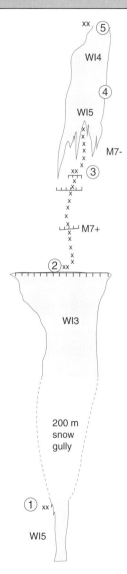

4) M7-, 45 m. Crank up a steep corner (six bolts) to gain the wild hanging daggers and steep ice above. Trend right past a sloping shelf to an ice belay at the base of the final tier.

5) WI5, 50 m. A final pitch of varied ice ends at a two bolt anchor on the left (may be difficult to find).

Descent Rappel the route.

Kicking Horse Canyon

The Kicking Horse Canyon boasts short approaches and sunny climbing with almost no avalanche hazard. Access is an issue because the approach involves walking along the train tracks, but people still seem to climb here without problems.

Approach Park at a plowed pullout on the north side of the Trans-Canada Highway just west of the westernmost bridge in the Kicking Horse Canyon. Cross the highway and descend under the bridge to the train tracks. Walk east along the tracks past *Riverview* (II WI2/3) and the

The upper 180 m of Jacob's Ladder.
Photo Dave Thomson.

Essondale climbs (WI3 and 4+) to the following three mixed routes.

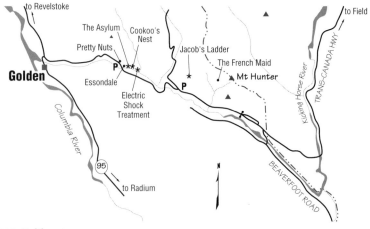

The Asylum IV M7 WI5, 170 m

Two discontinuous, parallel smears form on the big cliff to the right of the Essondale ice routes. *The Asylum* is the left-hand line that forms as a massive curtain dripping over slabby ice and mixed terrain. The last pitch has been climbed before as part of a route called The Halfway House, which traverses in from the left on rock.

Approach From the tracks hike through trees and up the gully below the route. If there is a well-trodden trail in the snow leading up to the Essondale climbs, follow that, then head right into the gully below *The Asylum*.

1-3) WI3 R or M4, 120 m. The "approach" pitches seem to form differently most years, but usually involve very thin ice that thickens the higher you climb. The first pitch can even have significant

Sean Isaac sending the crux of The Asylum *(pitch 4)*. *Photo Jim Gudjonson.*

Sean Isaac and Jim Gudjonson on pitch 4 of The Asylum. *Photo Black and White Productions.*

sections of rock with minimal gear. A few anchors (single bolts or pins) may be found depending on the line taken and the amount of ice coverage.

4) M7+, 25 m. Dry tool up the steep corner on the left edge of the cave and make a technical traverse out to the ice. Upon gaining the ice, only climb for a few metres, then traverse slightly right to a natural cave with a two bolt anchor. If this cave is completely covered with ice, then continue for 10 m up the ice to a sheltered stance behind the final pillar.

5) WI5, 30 m. Steep, sun-rotted ice to the top. Tree belay.

Descent Rappel the route from fixed rock anchors and Abalakovs.

Cookoo's Nest IV 5.8 R WI5, 180m

This is the right hand smear that forms less frequently. It is an excellent traditional route with marginal gear at the rock crux.

Approach The same as for *The Asylum*, but keep traversing right beneath that route into the gully below *Cookoo's Nest*.

Gear Standard mixed rack.

1) 5.6, WI3, 45 m. Grade 3 ice that doesn't quite reach the ground. There are usually a few ways of starting this pitch to reach the ice. The first ascent climbed a dirty corner and thin ice while the second ascent found easy ice the whole way.

2) WI3, 50 m. A full rope length of easy ice to a shelter screw belay under a little rock overhang.

The Asylum *left and* Cookoo's Nest *right from the Trans-Canada Highway. Photo Sean Isaac.*

Jim Gudjonson on the first ascent of Electric Shock Treatment. *Photo Brian Webster.*

3) 5.7, 15 m. Traverse up and left on easy rock splattered in ice from the big drip above. Belay in an alcove on ice.

4) 5.8 R, 20 m. Trend right across a quartzite slab with bad gear. Belay with gear in a crack on a little ledge beside a tree at the base of a prominent corner.

5) 5.8 WI5+, 40 m. Climb the nice corner above with good gear. Move left onto ice after about 10 m at a small ledge. If the ice is too thin, continue up the corner for another 10 m before moving left. Climb technical mushrooms and belay off ice.

Note A direct pitch to the upper ice was climbed at 5.10 from the belay at the top of pitch 3. It climbs out the roof above skipping the 5.8 R slab on pitch 4 and the 5.8 corner on pitch 5.

6) WI5+, 45 m. A sustained pitch of technical mushrooms and thin vertical ice. It gets progressively fatter and easier the higher you get.

Descent Either rappel the route from Abalakovs if the ice is fat or walk easily off right down through the trees.

Electric Shock Treatment 5.7 WI4, 20 m

A short, one-pitch mixed route located 5 m immediately right of the ice climb *Lobotomy* (II WI4).

Approach Continue along the train tracks about 600 m past *The Asylum*, then plow 20 minutes straight up to the route. Total time from the parking pullout is 40 minutes.

Gear Cams to 2" and ice screws.

Climb WI3 to the obvious traverse line left across an awkward fissure. Grade 4 ice leads to the trees at the top.

Descent Rappel from ice or trees.

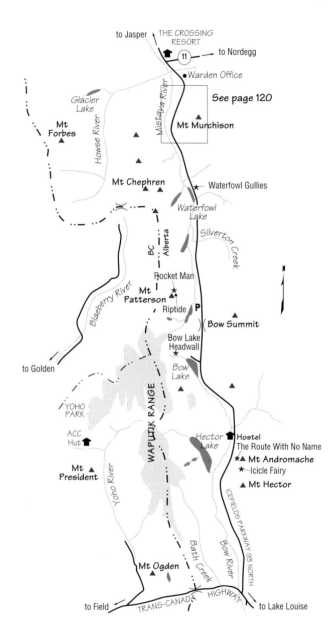

to Jasper

THE CROSSING RESORT

11

to Nordegg

● Warden Office

See page 120

Glacier Lake

Mt Forbes ▲

Howse River

Mistaya River

Mt Murchison ▲

Mt Chephren ▲

★ Waterfowl Gullies

Waterfowl Lake

Silverton Creek

BC Alberta

Blaeberry River

Rocket Man

Mt Patterson ▲★

Riptide

P

Bow Summit ▲

Bow Lake Headwall ★

to Golden

Bow Lake

YOHO PARK

WAPUTIK RANGE

ACC Hut

Hector Lake

Hostel
The Route With No Name

★▲ Mt Andromache

★ Icicle Fairy

▲ Mt Hector

Mt President ▲

Yoho River

Mt Ogden ▲

Bath Creek

Bow River

ICEFIELDS PARKWAY 93 NORTH

to Field

TRANS-CANADA HIGHWAY

to Lake Louise

Kim Csizmazia and Raphael Slawinski on The Icicle Fairy. *Photo Will Gadd.*

Mount Andromache

The Icicle Fairy III M6 WI4+, 70 m

This climb is situated on the south flank of Mount Andromache (the peak north of Mount Hector), and is easily visible from the road. A short section of overhanging, bolt-protected drytooling leads to a pitch of varied ice. Beware of avalanche prone slopes on the approach and above the route.

Approach Drive 21 km up the Icefields Parkway from its junction with the Trans-Canada Highway and park in a plowed pullout on the west side of the road. Hike up the drainage between Hector and Andromache (Hector Creek), and when level with the route traverse left (north) to the base. 1 hour.

1) M6, 40 m. Scramble up to a belay ledge at the base of steeper rock (bolt on the left). Make steep moves (M6) past three bolts to an ice blob and ledge behind a free-hanging dagger. Gently stem up behind the dagger past three more bolts and pull onto the front of the ice. Follow the ice strip above to a sheltered belay behind the upper pillar.

2) WI4+, 30 m. Climb steep ice to a two bolt belay on the right.

Descent Rappel the route using the bolt anchor atop pitch 2 and an Abalakov for pitch 1.

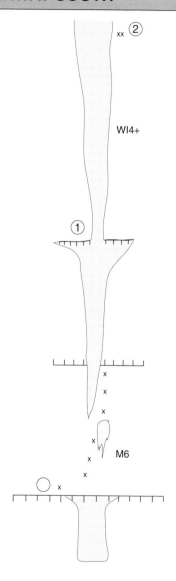

Route With No Name
V WI5+ R, 350 m

A semi-alpine route found high on the west face of Mount Andromache. The upper crux ice smear can be clearly seen from the highway while driving past. A definite early season route as there is "Big time avalanche terrain."

Approach Park on the side of the Icefields Parkway below the route just past the pullout for *The Icicle Fairy*. Hike up through the trees straight to the base of the wall. Go left to small breaks to gain a snow ledge. Traverse back right to the base of the route.

Gear Standard mixed rack.

Climbed in 8 pitches, the route follows gullies and snow-covered slabs to the upper 70 m ice smear. Begin at the base of two gullies: one straight-up (rappel anchors may be visible) and a less steep one angling right. Take the thinly iced right gully to rock slabs (single bolt anchor), then traverse back left for a pitch over easy rock to an alcove by a very steep wall. At this point, you are directly above the "straight-up" gully that was avoided. Descend a traversing snow ramp left past a steep, unformed icicle to another snow ramp that continues traversing left (now ascending). Tunnel underneath a large

The Route With No Name on the west face of Mount Andromache as seen from the Icefields Parkway. Photo Keith Haberl.

chockstone to a nice belay ledge. Keep sketching slabs and ledges trending right for three rope lengths until beneath the upper crux ice. Steep, thin ice (WI5+ R) with very little gear is climbed for a full rope length. A final 15 m section of WI4 completes the difficulties.

Descent Rappel the route from many bolt/piton stations.

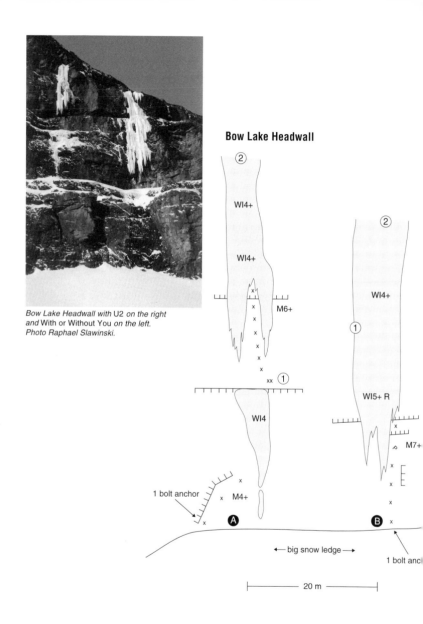

Bow Lake Headwall

② WI4+

WI4+

M6+

① WI4

WI5+ R

M7+

② WI4+

①

1 bolt anchor

M4+

A

B

← big snow ledge →

1 bolt anchor

├──── 20 m ────┤

Bow Lake Headwall with U2 *on the right and* With or Without You *on the left. Photo Raphael Slawinski.*

Bow Lake Headwall

The Bow Lake Headwall is now home to two aesthetic mixed lines. Both are multi-pitch endeavours within 50 m of one another and can be combined for a full day of climbing.

Approach Park at the Bow Glacier parking lot on the west side of the highway at the far end of Bow Lake near Num-ti-jah Lodge, 36.5 km north of the Trans-Canada Highway. Cross Bow Lake on foot or on skis. Stick to the trail along the right side of the lake if it is not frozen. From the far end of the lake follow a usually well-packed ski trail through the trees along the left side of a narrow canyon. Head across the moraine and into the broad amphitheatre where Bow Falls is located. *U2* and *With or Without You* can now be seen on the right-hand edge of the headwall. Hike up windblown moraine then traverse right across a ledge to the base of the routes. 2 hours. There is avalanche hazard on the slope below the routes but the routes themselves are safe.

Rob Owens on the first ascent of With or Without You (pitch 1). Photo Raphael Slawinski.

A With or Without You III M6+ WI4+, 65 m

The discontinuous line 50 m left of *Uli's Revenge.* The climbing is varied and surprisingly moderate.

1) M4+, 30 m. Start below a strip of ice on a steep slab (single bolt belay on the left). If the ice is well bonded, climb straight up the ice. If not, make a rising traverse from left to right past two bolts (M4+) to reach better ice and a two bolt belay on a ledge.

Rob Owens gunning for the ice on U2. Photo Roger Chayer.

2) M6+, 35 m. Dry tool past seven bolts (M6+) to the hanging ice. The last bolt is above the lip and may be covered in ice. There is another 25 m of WI4+ to the top.

Descent Rappel the route with double 50 m ropes: First from Abalakovs, then from the two bolt station at the top of pitch 1.

B U2 III M7+ WI5+ R, 60 m

This is the direct rock start to the (usually) unformed pillar of *Uli's Revenge*.

1) M7+, 30 m. Start directly below the hanging ice (single bolt belay) and dry tool past four bolts and a pin behind a block to a fragile dagger. Continue up detached vertical ice to better ice and a cave belay on the left.

2) WI4+, 30 m. A half-pitch of good ice leads to the top.

Descent One 60 m double rope rappel will reach the base of the route from an Abalakov at the top of pitch 2.

Mount Patterson

Rocket Man VI M7+ WI5+, 350 m

"A spectacular route in a high-energy environment!" *Rocket Man* is the series of smears and drips weeping down the steep cliff to the right of the Snowbird Glacier on Mount Patterson. It is in the same amphitheatre but opposite side as the infamous *Riptide* (VI WI6). Nine pitches of climbing make this the longest waterfall-style mixed route in the Rockies. Many hazards lurk below and above this route: active glaciers that spew debris threatening the approach; monstrous avalanche slopes below and above; and cornices that release chunks in the morning sun.

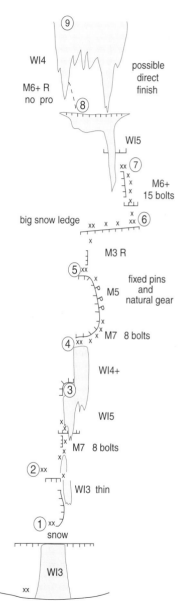

Approach Park at a pullout on the west side of Highway 93 about 7.3 km north of Bow Summit. The route should be obvious on the cliffs at the north end of the amphitheatre. From the pullout ski down and across the bottom of the valley and cross the river on snow bridges. Follow an open streambed to above the tree line. Continue between a pair of moraines trending right. Leave skis at the base of the huge slope under the climb, then slog up to the start of the ice. 2-2.5 hours.

Gear Quick draws for 15 bolts including long slings in addition to a standard mixed rack.

1) WI3, 50 m. From a belay on the left side of the ice, climb 25 m of ice, then wallow up the snow slope to a two bolt belay at a small rock band directly above. The bolts are on the left-hand side of the right-facing corner under a small roof and may be obscured by spindrift.

2) WI3 R, 50 m. Move right and then either climb a right-facing corner on thin ice with good natural gear or continue right and go up a steep snow slope to the bottom of the next icefall. Move left here and climb 10 m of thin ice that leads to a short steep pillar. At this juncture (before you climb the pillar) a single bolt is visible to the left. Move past it into a small alcove with a two bolt belay.

3) M7 WI5, 40 m. Climb the pillar, then move up and right into a small right-facing corner. The first two of eight bolts are on the left where the pillar thins out and there are three more on the face above and another three over the small roof up by the hanging dagger. From here 20 m of fairly steep ice leads to an ice belay at a roomy alcove.

The impressive Rocket Man *on Mount Patterson. Photo Raphael Slawinski.*

4) WI4+, 25 m. Move right from the alcove onto a steep curtain, then go straight up to a two bolt belay at the top right-hand side of the ice. A thinner and somewhat rotted ice flow, farther right, could also be attempted as a variation of pitch 5 and 6.

5) M7, 40 m. Move right from the belay and go up into a steep corner, then move right again to access a narrow vein of ice (eight bolts). Continue in a beautiful right-facing corner (M5) with narrow discontinuous cracks on the left-hand wall for pins and some small cams. Four pins were left in situ on the

lower section. There is also a bolt where the difficulties diminish at a small sloping ledge. Belay at a two bolt anchor on the left side of this ledge.

6) M3 R, 35 m. Continue up thin ice in the corner to a large snow-covered ledge that is steeper than it looks and loaded with loose rock. Clip a bolt if you can find it under the snow and move up and right past a two bolt belay at the base of the next cliff. Continue right past two more bolts to another two bolt belay on a snow ledge under a small roof.

7) M6+, 30 m. A pure rock pitch. Climb straight up the face into a large, right-facing corner and follow it to a two bolt belay on a ledge immediately right of the ice pillar. There are 15 bolts on this pitch. Rope drag is possible and it is recommended you reach back and unclip some of the draws while climbing.

8) WI5, 35 m. Move left onto the vertical pillar and climb good ice until it disappears under the snow on the next ledge. Tunnel up and left to a roomy alcove under the large roof and bash some pins in rotten rock for a belay.

9) M7-, 40 m. Move about 10 m left and climb 5 m of slightly overhanging rock with positive drytooling but no real pro to a small drip. Proceed up a WI4 to the top of the climb. A freestanding pillar may form on the right that would offer a WI6 finish.

Descent Rappel the route. Abalakovs on pitches 3, 8 and 9 and bolt stations for the rest. Do not rap off the belay at the bottom of pitch 7. Instead, traverse left to the alternate belay passed on the way up. For pitches 3 and 5 the first person down will have to clip some draws to access the belay and then pull the second in after.

Ben Firth inverted on Beer to Burn *in the One Ring Circus cave. Photo Rob Owens.*

Waterfowl Gullies

A great sport mixed area with awesome views of Howse Peak and Mount Chephren. Most of the routes are bolt protected and fairly short, so a bunch of draws, a few screws and a single 60 m rope will suffice. The threat of avalanches should only be an issue during times of high snowfall and extreme hazard; the slopes are usually clear of snow owing to its sunny exposure.

Approach Drive approximately 60 km up the Icefields Parkway and park on the west side of the road at a large plowed pullout (Waterfowl Lakes viewpoint), 18 km from the Bow Summit. There are three main gullies that are obvious from the road. One Ring Circus Gully is the farthest right. For this, hike up frozen scree directly above the parking area to a large cave near the top of the gully (45 minutes). For Finishing Hammer Gully, the middle of the three, hike up to the start of the ice in 15 minutes, and continue up an aesthetic WI3 gully to where it ends at a steep rock band with icicles pouring off of it. See topos for specific route details.

The One Ring Circus cave at the top of the gully. Photo Rob Owens.

One Ring Circus Gully

Routes described from left to right.

A Ain't Nobody Here But Us Chickens
M8, 25 m

Climb a steep wall on the left margin of the cave past two bolts into a groove. Make steep moves up and right past three more bolts to a hanging curtain. Continue up a hanging dagger clipping the sixth and final bolt from the ice. There is a two bolt station on the right side of the ledge.

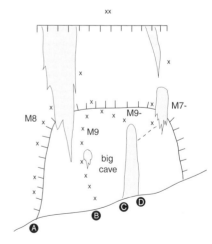

B Power to Burn M9, 25 m

Starting in the back of the cave, powerful climbing leads past a patch of ice to a horizontal crux past the down sloping lip of the cave. Finish on the *Chickens* dagger. Pre-clip the third bolt, as the bottom two are in very poor rock. Nine bolts.

C Beer to Burn M9-, 25 m

Climb to the top of a short pillar on the right side of the cave then punch it across a horizontal roof to join *Power to Burn*. Five bolts total including the last two of *Power to Burn*.

Scott DeCapio committing to the first ascent of Cornbread. Photo Will Gadd.

D Arriba M7, 25 m

An excellent, fully mixed route. Start up the same initial pillar as for *Beer to Burn*, then branch right to pull over a roof on the right side of the cave past two bolts. Continue up more ice and another rock step past a third bolt to a narrow vein and eventually the bolt station at the top of *Chickens*. It keeps getting harder as more ice disappears.

Cornbread M6, 25 m

A discontinuous smear on the right wall of the gully 100 m below the cave.

Gear Half dozen pitons, half set of nuts, 3" cam.

Climb either the thin ice directly or the rock corner on the left. Before committing to the upper tongue of ice locate a bomber 3" cam placement to the right.

Descent Single rope rappel from an Abalakov anchor.

The following two routes share the same start and are 40 m right of *Cornbread*. Both require standard mixed racks. Another WI3+ climb called *Meat Curtains* is to the right.

Angela's Ashes M5, 30 m

Climb rock to get to the dagger that hangs 4 m off of the deck.

This is the End Ever M5+ R, 30 m

Start up *Angela's Ashes*, then traverse left at half height to a extremely thin veneer. Gear is nominal from here but the ice gets thicker the higher you go.

Will Gadd on his desperate Power to Burn. *Photo Roger Chayer.*

Finishing Hammer Gully

Routes described from left to right.

A Money for Nothing and Your Picks for Free M8+, 30 m

Starting on a short flow on the left, make strenuous moves past five bolts to the left of two hanging pillars. Continue to a tree with slings on the left.

B Nine Inch Nails M8+ WI5 X, 30 m

Starting behind the right-hand hanging pillar, very technical drytooling past two bolts reaches the ice. The bolts would not prevent a ground fall from high on the stalactite. Continue to a tree with slings on the right.

C The Finishing Hammer M7+, 30 m

Starting on a stubby flow on the right, climb up and traverse left past three bolts to the hanging pillar. Continue to a tree on the right.

Finishing Hammer Gully. Photo Raphael Slawinski.

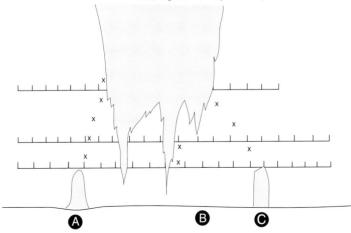

Mount Murchison— Transparent Fool Area

Approach Park at a plowed pullout on the east side of Highway 93, 24.5 km north of Bow Summit. Walk back (south) along the road to the obvious drainage that is Bison Creek. The routes are visible on a rock band near the end of the valley. Follow the creek to the routes, skirting a narrow canyon by ascending slopes on the left, then dropping back into the creek bottom above the impasse. 1.5 hours.

The routes are not threatened by avalanches but the approach can be dangerous during times of high hazard.

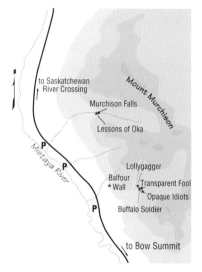

Opaque Idiots 5.8 WI4 (M5), 50 m

A small tongue of ice that occasionally seeps from half way up the cliff to the right of *The Transparent Fool* (WI5, 50 m).

Gear Cams to 3.5", nuts, screws.

A good crack is climbed to reach the ice, then a 5.6 chimney is climbed to the top of the cliff.

The following two routes are located on either side of the lower tier of *Bison Falls* (WI3).

Buffalo Soldier M7, 15 m

Technical rock with sloping holds reaches a big roof and a short bit of ice near the far right side of the broad flow (five bolts).

Lollygagger M6, 15 m

Three bolts on the left edge of *Bison Falls* reaches a narrow vein of ice.

Jim Gudjonson stretching out on Buffalo Soldier.
Photo Sean Isaac.

Mount Murchison—Balfour Wall

Approach The ice flows of *Balfour Wall* can be seen through the trees on the lowest cliff immediately left of the Bison Creek drainage. Hike through the trees and up to the routes in 30 minutes. There is zero avalanche hazard.

Beavis M7, 10 m
The left-hand of two bolted mixed lines (four bolts).

Butthead M6+, 10 m
The right-hand route. Three bolts worth of rock then step right onto the ice.

Descent Either rappel from trees or walk off via a gully on the right.

Jim Gudjonson on Lollygagger. *Photo Sean Isaac.*

Murchison Falls Area

Approach Park on the side of the highway, 27.5 km north of Bow Summit, where an obvious drainage crosses the road. Begin by hiking up the drainage then, confronted by short rock steps, move up onto the left bank and follow it to the open amphitheatre with Murchison Falls in the back.

Lessons of Oka III 5.7 WI4, 70 m
This fine route is located 200 m right of Murchison Falls in an obvious left-facing rock corner with smears of thin ice.

Climb the mixed corner and ice above. Another thin ice/mixed route just right of *Lessons of Oka* called *Zapatista Liberation* (III WI5, 90 m) occasionally forms.

Descent Rappel the route.

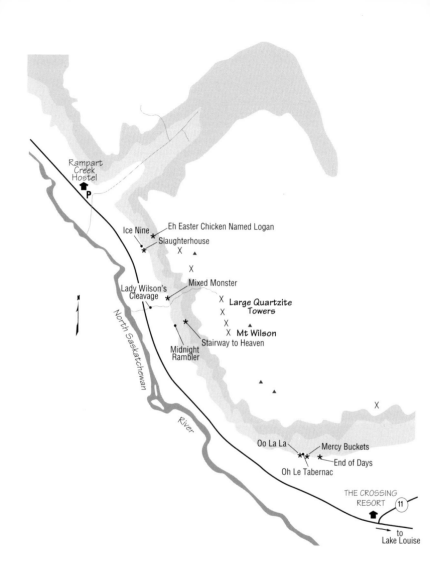

Rampart
Creek
Hostel
P

Ice Nine ✳ Eh Easter Chicken Named Logan
✳ Slaughterhouse
X ▲

X

Mixed Monster
Lady Wilson's
Cleavage ✳
X **Large Quartzite**
X **Towers**
X
✳ X ▲ **Mt Wilson**
X
Midnight Stairway to Heaven
Rambler

North Saskatchewan

▲

▲ ▲

River

X

Oo La La Mercy Buckets
✳✳ ✳ End of Days
Oh Le Tabernac

THE CROSSING
RESORT ⑪

→
to
Lake Louise

MOUNT WILSON

Mount Wilson looms over Saskatch-ewan River Crossing as a hulking mass of snow, ice and rock. Its many gullies and amphitheatres are home to some of the best mixed climbing in the Rockies. Both multi-pitch testpieces and single pitch sport routes abound. All the routes are south facing and enjoy sun all winter. In fact, it sometimes gets so hot that mixed climbing in a T-shirt or even no shirt is possible. All these routes are threatened by miles of prime avalanche real estate.

End Of Days III 5.7 WI4+, 55 m

This route is the left of two drips found on the cliffs right (south) of *Oh Le Tabernac*, between it and another estab-lished ice line called *The Shining No-bodies* (WI3, 40 m). The other potential line that formed about 100 m to the right was "deemed too difficult and has been left to future generations." The difficulty being the amount of choss cleaning it would take to forge a route to the ice!

Approach Park on the side of the high-way 2.5 km north of the Saskatchewan River Crossing. Hike through open for-est then up the drainage descending from *Oh Le Tabernac*. Before reaching *Oh Le Tabernac*, cut right and follow the base of the cliff to the route. 1 hour.

1) 5.7 R, 30 m. Rock climb past six widely spaced bolts (drilled on lead) to a two bolt belay under a roof.

2) WI4+, 25 m. Steep yet plastic ice ends at a tree belay.

Descent Double 60 m ropes will reach the ground from the tree on top.

Tabernac Wall

To the left of *Oh Le Tabernac* (WI5+), two awesome ice curtains separated by very steep rock form to create the 2-pitch *Oo La La*. *Mercy Buckets* is a single pitch, moderate warm-up to the right that gets completely covered in ice later in the season. Both routes have two bolt anchors for convenient single 60 m rope rappels. This area faces directly south and therefore is pleasantly warm when sunny. However, this also increases the chance of avalanches from the huge bowls above.

Approach Park on the side of the high-way 2.5 km north of the Saskatchewan River Crossing. Hike through open for-est then up the drainage descending from *Oh Le Tabernac*. 45 minutes.

A Oo La La M8, 50 m

1) M8, 30 m. Stick clip the third bolt, then get prepared to "pull down" as steep, powerful moves lead out a roof to a vertical wall and hanging drips. There are 10 bolts and a two bolt anchor on the large ice ledge half way up the wall. A short length of chain hangs from the fourth bolt to facilitate an easier clip. Beware of the protruding block on the ledge below while making clips. It would hurt if you blew a clip and landed on it.

2) M7+, 30 m. Vertical rock with two cruxy roofs protected by 11 bolts lead to 5 m of ice and a two bolt anchor.

B Mercy Buckets M6+, 25 m

Seven bolts on vertical rock to ice and a two bolt anchor on an ice ledge half way up the right side of *Oh Le Tabernac*.

Lady Wilson's Cleavage Amphitheatres

The steep rock amphitheatres on either side of *Lady Wilson's Cleavage* (WI3) hold bolted multi-pitch testpieces.

Stairway to Heaven IV M7+ WI5, 95 m

An awesome 3-pitch line with back-to-back M7+ pitches. For a full day linkup covering tons of terrain, try to combine *Midnight Rambler* (WI3, 150 m), *Stairway to Heaven* (M7+ WI5, 95 m) and *Living in Paradise* (WI6+, 160 m), which is located directly above *Stairway to Heaven*. This is avalanche country and the terrain is massive so heads up on conditions.

Approach Park on the highway 8 km past Saskatchewan River Crossing. The route's hanging icicle (usually broken off) will be visible high above, two amphitheatres to the right of *Lady Wilson's Cleavage* (WI3). *Midnight Rambler* is the narrow flow of ice seen through the trees below the amphitheatre. Bushwhack through the trees and cut into the drainage descending from *Midnight Rambler*, which is climbed to the base of *Stairway to Heaven*. 2 hours including *Midnight Rambler*.

1) WI5, 20 m. Gun up a short, burly pillar to a two bolt belay on the left.

2) M7+, 27m. A pure rock pitch that pulls out two roofs. There is a total of 12 bolts to reach a two bolt anchor on a compact ledge.

Oh Le Tabernac *with* Oo La La *tackling the drips on the left and* Mercy Buckets *gaining the ice on the right. Photo Raphael Slawinski.*

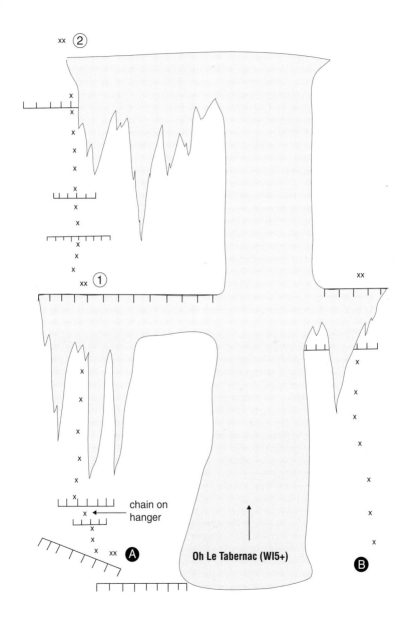

chain on
hanger

Oh Le Tabernac (WI5+)

Sean Isaac cutting loose on Oo La La.
Photo Freddie Snalam.

Dave Thomson and Kefira Allen on Stairway
to Heaven. *Photo Joe Josephson.*

Eamonn Walsh on-sighting Oo La La. *Photo Dave Thomson.*

3) M7+ WI4, 50 m. Sustained overhanging dry tooling past six bolts leads to the hanging icicle that can be stemmed to relieve flaming arms. If the ice is broken off at the lip, expect the transition from rock to ice to be harder. Continue to the top on easy angled ice.

Descent Rappel the route. From the top, rappel from Abalakov to just above the ice roof and set another Abalakov that will allow a double 60 m rope rappel to the base of the route. *Midnight Rambler* is descended by rappelling from trees and/or ice anchors.

Mixed Monster IV M8 WI5, 120 m

An impressive drip separated from the ground by 50 m of high quality, overhanging rock. There is serious avalanche hazard above this route and slides usually start rocketing off the top around noon when the sun is at its most intense. Be sure to reach the base of the climb and the relative protection of the rock overhangs before things get active. Better yet, wait for a cloudy day.

Approach Park 9.5 km past Saskatchewan River Crossing, then hike through open forest and up the right side of the gully that descends from the climb.

1) WI3, 15 m. Climb the easy initial ice blob to a two bolt anchor. Depending on the year, the ice may be higher, hence covering the anchor. In this case, belay from screws or one of the protection bolts on the next pitch.

2) M6+, 25 m. A long, pure rock pitch past 13 bolts with the crux out roofs at the end.

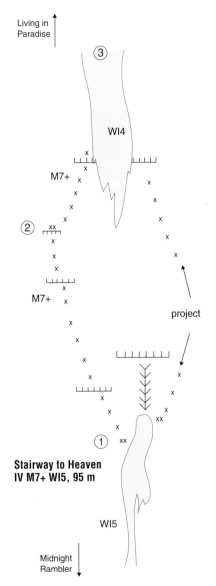

Living in Paradise

③

WI4

M7+

②

M7+

project

Stairway to Heaven
IV M7+ WI5, 95 m

①

WI5

Midnight Rambler

3) M7+, 12m. Another pitch of pure rock (six bolts). Short but technical. Climbed with ice tools and rock shoes on the first ascent, subsequent ascents have resorted to more "traditional" techniques by using crampons.

4) M8 WI5, 45 m. Traverse right out the big roof to snag the hanging ice curtain. Continue up steep ice to the top.

Descent A walk off to the right and into *Lady Wilson's Cleavage* is possible but not recommended. Instead, rappel from an Abalakov at the top to a point near the lip of the roof where the ice curtain hangs off. Set another Abalakov, which will reach the top of the initial ice blob with double 60 m ropes.

Right: Kafira Allen dwarfed by Mixed Monster. *Photo Dave Thomson.*
Below: Dave Thomson on the crux of Mixed Monster *(pitch 4). Photo Sean Isaac.*

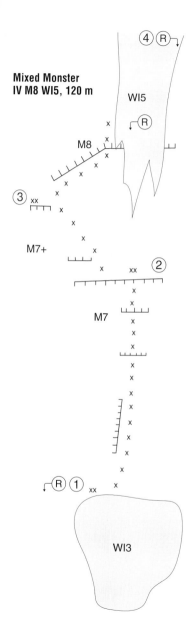

Mixed Monster
IV M8 WI5, 120 m

④ ®

WI5

®

M8
x x
x
x
x
x x
x
x

③ xx
x

x

M7+
x
x xx ②

x
x
M7
x
x
x
x
x
x
x
x
x

x

® ① xx x

WI3

Ice Nine Wall

The steep amphitheatre behind the first pitch of *Ice Nine* (WI6) contains a bolted mixed route with sunny exposure.

Approach Park on the highway 11.3 km north of the Saskatchewan River Crossing and about 1 km before (south) of Rampart Creek Hostel. Hike through the trees and into the drainage that leads steeply to the route. A huge avalanche bowl above threatens the route.

Slaughterhouse M8+, 30 m

This route sports immaculate, horizontally stratified rock providing superb drytooling to reach the back side of *Ice Nine*. There are nine bolts with the last one at the lip of the roof protecting the

The super steep Slaughterhouse *behind* Ice Nine.
Photo Geoff Trump.

overhanging and awkward ice moves pulling around to the front of the curtain. The difficulty of the route will change as the ice fills out; eventually allowing you to skip the final crux and step directly onto the ice. Beware that *Ice Nine* is notorious for suddenly collapsing near the end of the season.

Eh Spring Chicken Named Logan
V 5.8 R WI5, 500 m

This is the mixed gully system located high above *Ice Nine*.

Approach Park as for *Ice Nine/Slaughter House*. Either climb *Ice Nine* or scramble via low-angled rock ledges on the far left to tree line (good bivy sites). 3 to 5 hours depending on snow conditions.

Begin 50 m to the left of the main ridge and climb 150 m of 5.6 alpine rock to reach a large ledge. This section can be done in 3-4 pitches, first staying in broken corners then an easy slab and finally trending left and up to exit corner. Traverse the ledge right into the main ice gully that is climbed for 300 m past several WI3 steps. The crux is the last step involving 5.8 choss to gain a "wobbly" WI5 pillar.

Descent Rappel and down climb the upper snow and ice gully, then rappel the lower rock section just right (climber's right) of the ascent route. This is done in three 60 m raps with the first from trees on the ledge and the next two from single bolt anchors.

Sean Isaac stems to the ice on the first ascent of Slaughterhouse. *Photo Roger Chayer.*

WEEPING WALL

The Snakes and Ladders area consists of two traditional routes located on a broken outcropping a couple kilometres before the *Polar Circus* gully.

Approach This area is located 2 km south of *Polar Circus*. Park on the side of the Icefields Parkway and hike through trees for 45 minutes to the base of the ice. A WI2 flow finishes at some trees. Continue up a 5.6 corner and fourth class terrain to the base of the following two routes.

Gear Standard mixed rack for both routes described below.

Pee Bottle Matters M4, 30 m
The left-hand line. Climb ledgy rock for 12 m to a small roof then step left onto thin ice.

Empty Bladders M7, 30 m
The right-hand line. The first ascensionists suggest it may live up to its name if the gear is not preplaced. Climb easy ice to a ledge then bust out the roof past a couple of fixed pins to the hanging dagger.

The Blender IV 5.9/M5 WI4, 250 m
Similar in length and style to *Mixed Master* but went unrecorded, *The Blender* tackles the rock wall to the left of *Polar Circus*. It features hard snowed-up rock climbing and thin smears that weep from cracks. The route only ascends the lower portion of the wall to where it noticeably kicks back to a lesser angle.

Approach Park 15 km north of the Rampart Creek Hostel. Located left of *Polar Circus* is a large left-facing dihedral capped by a roof at 30 m with a WI 2-3 weep flowing from it. This is the first large piece of ice left by the bypass ice for the grade 4 pitch of *Polar Circus* and is at the same elevation. *The Blender* begins about left of this under the right edge of a large terrace 80 m up the wall.

Gear Standard mixed rack with extra small to medium cams. Be prepared to leave some pins and other gear to back up rappel anchors.

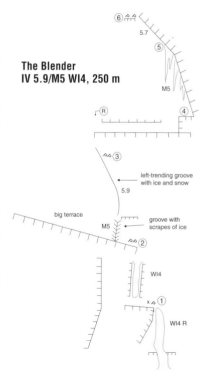

The Blender
IV 5.9/M5 WI4, 250 m

M5

5.7

M5

left-trending groove with ice and snow

5.9

big terrace

groove with scrapes of ice

M5

WI4

WI4 R

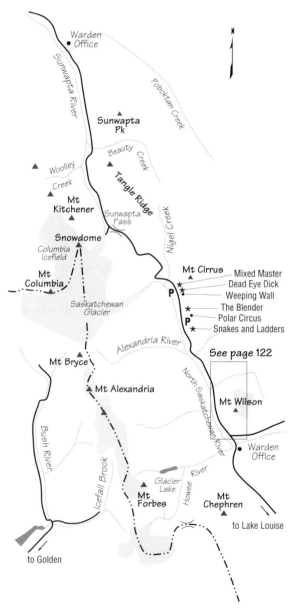

Warden
Office

Sunwapta River

Poboktan Creek

Sunwapta
Pk

Beauty Creek

Woolley

Creek

Tangle Ridge

Mt
Kitchener

Sunwapta
Pass

Nigel Creek

Snowdome

Columbia
Icefield

Mt
Columbia

Saskatchewan
Glacier

Mt Cirrus — Mixed Master
P ★ — Dead Eye Dick
★ — Weeping Wall
★ — The Blender
P — Polar Circus
★ — Snakes and Ladders

Alexandria River

See page 122

Mt Bryce

Mt Alexandria

North Saskatchewan River

Mt Wilson

Warden
Office

Bush River

Icefall Brook

Glacier
Lake

Howse River

Mt
Forbes

Mt
Chephren

to Golden

to Lake Louise

1) WI3, 50 m. Climb a thin sheet of ice that flows from a chimney on the right side of the large terrace 80 m up the wall. Follow this ice to a ledge and a fixed rock anchor.

2) WI4, 30 m. Climb the iced up chimney to the terrace.

3) 5.9/M5, 50 m. Walk left along the terrace 5-10 m until there is a break/groove in the overhanging wall above. Climb the icy groove to a mantle onto a big flake. Follow the left-trending groove that cuts the slab above to a fixed rock anchor below the prominent ledge.

4) 5.6, 50 m. Move up to the ledge and make your way right past a "heinous belly crawl" into the base of the large left-facing, left-leaning corner.

5) 5.9/M5, 50 m. Climb the leaning corner with plenty of opportunities for good gear until you have had enough.

6) 5.7, 20 m. Finish the corner/slab onto easy ground and a ledge with a fixed pin anchor.

Descent Rappel the upper slab in two raps to the top of the 3 pitch, then follow the route to the bottom. You should find the anchors for the last two raps but maybe not the middle two.

Dead Eye Dick IV 5.10b WI5+ R/X, 100 m

A rarely formed line that streams down the compact cliff immediately left of the *Lower Weeping Wall*. In the winter of '99/00, it formed fat right to the ground and received numerous ascents at WI4.

Approach Park at the *Weeping Wall* parking area on the west side of the Icefields Parkway, 16.9 km north of the Rampart Creek Hostel.

Gear Standard mixed rack.

1) 5.10, 30 m. Climb a right-facing corner on the left side of the ice to a hanging belay on gear at the top of the corner.

2-4) WI5 R/X, 100 m. Traverse right 4 m to gain the main flow and follow ice of variable thickness ranging from thin to very thin.

Descent Rappel the route from Abalakovs if the ice is thick enough. If not, slog over right to the top of *Snivelling Gully*, which is easily rappelled.

Mixed Master IV 5.8 WI5, 300 m

The original mixed classic! At the time, a cutting edge route that set the standard for mixed climbing in the '90s. You can't beat six pitches of quality mixed climbing, only 10 minutes from the road. Some new bolt anchors have been installed in different places than the original ascent but they seem more logical.

Approach Park at the *Weeping Wall* parking area on the west side of the Icefields Parkway, 16.9 km north of the Rampart Creek Hostel. Walk north along the road for a couple hundred metres, then head up to the base of the route, which should be obvious in a big corner/gully system just above the road. 10 minutes.

Gear Standard mixed rack.

1) WI4, 50 m. Climb a thin apron of low-angled ice past an old fixed rock belay on the left. Continue up the corner via a narrow pillar of ice to a two bolt anchor at a stance on the left about 5 m from where the angle eases off and the snow ledge starts.

2) WI3, 30 m. Climb the last steep bit of ice and continue up to the top to the snow bowl where a two bolt anchor will be found in the steep rock wall above.

3) WI2, 40 m. Traverse up and right along the snow ledge and climb a short flow of gentle ice through some bushes to a belay stance in a left-facing corner.

4) 5.8, 40 m. Traverse left from the belay on rock with good protection to a groove. Scratch up the groove (crux) to a snow arete and a fixed rock anchor at the base of a thinly iced left-facing corner.

5) M4, 40 m. Climb the mixed corner and a 1 m rock step at the top exiting right to a tree belay.

6) Snow, 60 m. Cruise up the snow slope and belay at a two bolt anchor on the right of the final ice.

7) WI5, 40 m. Hook up a thin vein of ice (crux) to gain the fatter waterfall above. If the vein is not properly formed, move right and climb rock (5.8) to bypass the lower section.

Descent Rappel the route from bolt anchors. From the top of pitch 4, rappel straight down the main gully to a bolt anchor on the right wall. Another rap deposits you at the snow ledge on pitch 2.

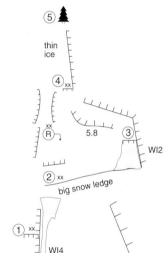

Joe Buszowski hooks thin ice on the last pitch of Mixed Master *during its first ascent. Photo Troy Kirwan.*

DAVID THOMPSON HIGHWAY

Forgotten Land IV M6 WI5, 170 m

A great climb that has only formed once. If formed, it will be obvious from the highway in the middle of the cliff band on the right side of *Two O'clock Falls* (III WI2-3, 120 m).

Approach Park 29.5 km past the Saskatchewan River Crossing on the David Thompson Highway. Hike directly to the route through forest. 1 hour.

Gear Standard mixed rack.

1) 5.8, 40 m. Climb a right-facing corner past a small roof for 20 m (possible belay in corner), then move out left making an easy rock traverse to gain a ledge. Follow the ledge right to a one bolt rock anchor.

2) M6, 50 m. Directly above, a straight-in crack with thin ice decorating the sides of it is climbed to a roof. Clip a bolt and pull the roof on the right reaching thin ice. Continue up little pillars to a sheltered ice belay below a rock overhang.

3-4) WI4 and 5, 80 m. From the belay, traverse right on steep icicles then go straight up fatter ice.

Descent An easy walk off to the right or rappel the route.

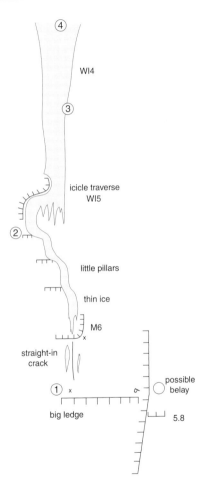

David Thompson Highway 135

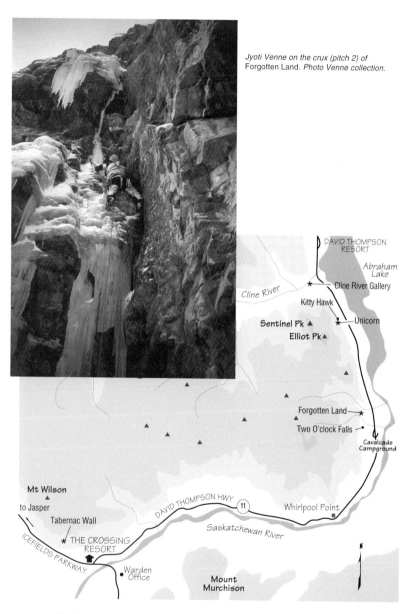

Jyoti Venne on the crux (pitch 2) of Forgotten Land. *Photo Venne collection.*

DAVID THOMPSON RESORT

Abraham Lake

Cline River

★ Cline River Gallery

Kitty Hawk

✶ Unicorn

Sentinel Pk ▲

Elliot Pk ▲

▲

▲

Forgotten Land —★

Two O'clock Falls —●

Cavalcade Campground

▲

▲

▲

Mt Wilson
▲
to Jasper

Tabernac Wall

DAVID THOMPSON HWY (11) Whirlpool Point ■

★ THE CROSSING RESORT

Saskatchewan River

ICEFIELDS PARKWAY

● Warden Office

Mount Murchison

N

Unicorn IV M7-, 80 m

A beautiful 2 pitch mixed route that has a little bit of everything: a traditional pitch and a well-protected bolted pitch. Unfortunately, it only seems to form once every few years.

Approach From the Saskatchewan River Crossing on the Icefields Parkway (Highway 93 north), drive north on the David Thompson Highway (Highway 11) for 38.4 km, then park on the side of the road. The route is located immediately left of *Kitty Hawk* (WI5) in the farthest right of three prominent gullies on Elliot Peak. 1 hour. There is a large bowl above that threatens this route.

Gear Standard mixed rack.

1) M7-, 45 m. Climb patches of thin ice and blobs to an overhanging corner that takes good cams. Pull left onto a 1 m rock step (M7-) and up grade 5 ice to a two bolt anchor on a good ledge.

2) M7-, 35 m. Dry tool past seven bolts (M7-) to an ice curtain (WI5).

Descent Rappel the route.

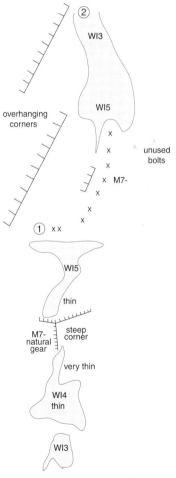

Eric Dumerac on pitch 2 of the Unicorn *with* Kitty Hawk *on the right. Photo Dave Thomson.*

Cline River Gallery

Approach Park at the Pinto Creek trailhead 42.5 km from the Icefields Parkway on the west side of the Cline River bridge. From the back of the old gravel quarry pick up the popular summer hiking trail. Follow this for about 15 minutes to a grove of poplar trees. A few hundred metres into the grove, the trail will begin to go up hill. As it does so a small hill rises on the left behind which is a faint draw. Either follow the draw through the bush or hike along its upper left shoulder (flagged) to a broad open hillside descending to the river. Go down the hill and locate a dry gully through the cliffs that will deposit you at the edge of the river and the base of the climbs. 30 minutes.

The two mixed routes are found on the rock wall between the easy (WI3) ramp on the left and the steep pillar of *Pure Energy* (WI4+) on the right. They are described from right to left.

Evil Energy M6, 25 m

A bolted line (six bolts) that links rock sections with wings of ice that branch off of the left side of *Pure Energy*.

Pure Joy M5, 25 m

A natural line left of *Evil Energy* that climbs blobs of ice splattered on compact rock. One bolt was drilled on lead before exiting onto the ice curtain at the top.

Gear One bolt, half dozen pitons (KBs to shallow angles), screws.

MacBeth IV M6 WI5, 200 m

This rarely formed climb can be seen from the highway on a rise east of the David Thompson Resort in the fourth major gully system on Mount Stelfox going east.

Approach Drive into Mackenzies Trails West on the north side of the highway just across from the David Thompson Resort. Take the first left fork or park at the junction. Proceed east to a water storage tank and open pond. Cross around to the other side and follow a trail for five minutes to a junction. Follow the north fork (right) for another five minutes, then head east gaining elevation up the slope to where a creekbed/wash opens up and leads to the base of the route. 50 minutes.

Gear Standard mixed rack.

Five short steps of WI4/5 deposit you at the base of the crux pitch. Climb thin ice and mixed for 20 m, then pull through the roof (M6) past a fixed pin out left to gain the main flow. Another 40 m of rambling ice leads to a final 20 m pillar (WI4).

Descent Rappel the route from Abalakovs and trees until at the base of the crux pitch, then down climb and traverse left onto the slope east of the creekbed where easy walking will get you out.

WAD Valley

WAD Valley, an acronym for the names of the first climbers to discover it (Wes, Andrew and Dave), boasts warm, sunny exposure and two fine mixed lines. This only scratches the surface of the great potential that the Jasper area holds for new mixed routes.

Approach From Jasper, drive along Highway 16 east toward Edmonton. At the signed turn-off for Jasper Park Lodge, turn right and cross the bridge over the Athabasca River. Turn left onto Maligne Lake Road and drive along Medicine Lake, parking on the side of the road 3 km past Summit Lake/Jaques Lake trailhead. WAD Valley is the third major drainage past the trailhead. Do not approach via the creekbed itself as there is a small waterfall blocking the way. Instead, hike up the left side of the drainage to where a sparsely treed ridge comes down from the left. Follow this up to the main, open ridge and continue until it flattens out. Traverse right through thin trees to the creekbed. From this point the creekbed can be followed directly to the climbs. The first climb you reach is a WI5+ pillar named *Softly, Softly, Cagey Monkey* followed by the wide *Boss Hog* (WI4). The two mixed routes described below are to the right. There is rarely avalanche danger as the area is quite dry but rockfall is a potential hazard from the scree slopes above. 1 hour.

Spanish Fly WI4+ 5.9, 30 m

Begin up low-angled ice immediately right of *Boss Hog*, then launch up a steep, chandeliered pillar to a rock roof. Three bolts protect the moves out the roof to a chain anchor.

Fire Drake M6 WI5+, 35 m

Fire Drake is located 30 m right of *Spanish Fly*. Ten metres of mixed rock and ice lead to a roof and the steep pillar above. Two bolts protect the mixed section but bring some pins along to supplement them.

Descent Rappel from Abalakov or trees.

Fire Drake *in WAD Valley. Photo Rob Owens.*

ROUTE INDEX

FA = first ascent
FFA = first free ascent
FMA = first mixed ascent
FRA = first recorded ascent

104 Cookoo's Nest IV 5.8 R WI5, 180 m, FA: Larry Dolecki, Jim Gudjonson, February 1997.

117 Cornbread M6, 25 m, FA: Scott DeCapio, Kelly Cordes, December 1999.

 97 Coyotes III 5.9 WI5, 50 m, FA: Allan Massin, Steve Pratt, February 1998.

 94 Cragganmore IV 5.8 WI4, 200 m, FA: Jim Gudjonson, Gord Ross, March 1997.

 71 Day After les Vacances de Monsieur Hulot, The V 5.10+ M7 WI6, 270 m,
     FA: Francois Damilano, Joe Josephson, March 1994. FFA: Matt Collins,
     Raphael Slawinski, April 1997.

 91 Dead Dog Cafe IV M6 WI5, 55 m, FA: Jim Gudjonson, Brian Webster, March 1998.

133 Dead Eye Dick IV 5.10b WI5+ R/X, 100 m, FA: Karen McNeill, Dave Thomson, December 1995.

 17 Deviant, The II 5.6 WI5, 35 m, FA: Joe Josephson, Brad Wrobleski, January 1995.

 87 Dick Jones M7-, 15 m, FA: Sean Isaac, Roger Strong, March 2000.

 59 Dog Fight IV M7 WI6+ X, 50 m, FA: Kafira Allen, Dave Thomson, March 1998.

 87 Don't Mess With Da Nest M7, 10 m, FA: Kim Csizmazia, Will Gadd, Guy Lacelle,
     December 1999.

 43 Double Dutch M7, 20 m, FA: Sean Isaac, March 1998.

 31 Dr. Evil IV 5.6 WI5 R, 75 m, FA: Jeff Everett, Raphael Slawinski, October 1999.

 56 Egypt M7+ 20 m, FA: Dave Thomson, January 2000.

130 Eh Spring Chicken Named Logan V 5.8 R WI5, 500 m, FA: Dave Marra, Eamonn Walsh, April 2000.

105 Electric Shock Treatment 5.7 WI4, 20 m, FA: Jim Gudjonson, Brian Webster, February 1998.

 27 EMF IV A0 WI6, 120 m, FA: Dave Campbell, Jeff Everett, Bob Lee, December 1995.

131 Empty Bladders M7, 30 m, FA: Cory Balano, Dave Edgar, Dave Marra, March 2000.

123 End Of Days III 5.7 WI4+, 55 m, FA: Deborah Lantz, Dave Thomson, Tom Wolfe, January 2000.

138 Evil Energy M6, 25 m, FA: Mike Adolf, Todd Learn, February 2000.

 59 Extended Mix V M5 WI4+, 400 m, FA: Steve DeMaio, Raphael Slawinski, April 1998.

 67 Extreme Comfort V 5.11 R A3 WI6, 180 m, FA: Conrad Anker, Scott Backes, Joe Josephson, April 1995.

 88 Fantasy Shower M7+, 30 m, FA: Dave Thomson, March 1997.

 92 Fat Tire II 5.8 WI4 R, 95 m, FA: Cory Balano, Dave Edgar, Jeff Lemieux, Dave Marra,
     December 1999.

 77 Fiasco V M8-/5.12a WI5+, 170 m, FA: Sean Isaac, Dave Thomson, February 1998.

119 Finishing Hammer, The M7+, 30 m, FA: Will Gadd, Raphael Slawinski, December 1999.

139 Fire Drake M6 WI5+, 35 m, FA: Ken Wallator and partner mid-1990s. FFA: Gary Boyd,
     Paul Valiulis, 1997/1998.

 83 Flake Route, The M5, 15 m, FA: unknown

 63 Fleshlumpeater IV M6 WI5+, 90 m, FA: Sean Isaac, Dave Thomson, March 1997.

135 Forgotten Land IV M6 WI5, 170 m, FA: Allan Massin, Steve Pratt, February 1997.

 60 French Connection, The M4+ WI4, 400 m, FA: Chris Geilser (solo), April 1998.

 66 French Reality V 5.8 WI6+, 150 m, FA: Claude Blazy, Francois Damilano, Philippe Pibarot, March 1992.

 67 French Toast V M7 WI5+ R, 130 m, FA: Sean Isaac, Dave Thomson, November 1997.

 77 General Malaise IV M6 WI5, 90 m, FA: Jim Gudjonson, Sean Isaac, Brian Webster, April 2000.

87 Gong Show, The M8+/M9-, 10 m, FA: Ben Firth, January 2000.

26 Green Man Gronks III 5.9 M6, 45 m, FA: Eric Dumerac, Sean Isaac, February 1999.

57 Gunfighter, The II 5.10+ WI3 R, 50 m, FA: Cory Balano, Tyler Freed, December 1998.

81 Half 'n' Half M6+, 20 m, FA: Sean Isaac, December 1997.

83 Half a Gronk M5+, 15 m, FA: Eric Dumerac, Guy Edwards, January 1998.

93 Home Brew IV 5.10 WI5, 60 m, FA: Larry Stanier, Grant Statham, December 1996
FFA: unknown.

26 Hovering Half Breed M7+, 30 m, FA: Steve DeMaio, Raphael Slawinski,
Ken Wylie, November 1997.

108 Icicle Fairy, The III M6 WI4+, 70 m, FA: Kim Csizmazia, Will Gadd, Raphael Slawinski,
November 1999.

84 In Reverse M7, 15 m, FA: Sean Isaac, December 1999.

101 Jacob's Ladder IV M7+ WI5, 200 m, FA: Kefira Allen, Dave Thomson, March 1998.

93 Just Water III 5.10 WI5, 55 m, FA: Allan Massin, Toby "the Australian," March 1998.

95 Last Call M7- WI5, 45 m, FA: Sean Isaac, Dave Thomson, December 1997.

121 Lessons of Oka III 5.7 WI4, 70 m, FA: Ken Wallator, Brian Webster, February 1991.

120 Lollygagger M6, 15 m, FA: Jim Gudjonson, Sean Isaac, February 2000.

98 Lone Pine III 5.7 WI5, 55 m, FA: Allan Massin, Steve Pratt, February 1998.
FFA: Greg Thaczuk, Eamonn Walsh, December 1999.

138 MacBeth IV M6 WI5, 200 m, FA: Mike Adolf, Joe Jesse, December 1999.

24 Magic Touch II WI3 R 5.8, 50 m, FA: Janet Brygger, Anthony Nielson, November 1996.

99 Margaritaville III M7, 70 m, FA: Jim Gudjonson, Nicole Gudjonson, December 1999.

92 McNalley's M6, 25 m, FA: Jim Gudjonson, Pete Oxtoby, Tim Styles, December 1997.

42 Mental Jewelry M6+, 12 m, FA: Janet Brygger, Anthony Nielson, January 1997.

124 Mercy Buckets M6+, 25 m, FA: Dave Thomson, Tom Wolfe, January 2000.

83 Minimal Impact M5+, 20 m, FA: Guy Lacelle, Geoff Powter, December 1999.

133 Mixed Master IV 5.8 WI5, 300 m, FA: Joe Buszowski, Troy Kirwan, December 1991.

127 Mixed Monster IV M8 WI5, 120 m, FA: Sean Isaac, Dave Thomson, February 1998.

81 Mojo M8+, 20 m, FA: Simon Parson, December 1999.

61 Mon Ami V 5.6 WI4+, 150 m, FA: Serge Angelucci, Allan Massin, February 1989.

119 Money for Nothing and Your Picks for Free M8+, 30 m, FA: Joe Buszowski, Dave Dornian,
Will Gadd, Raphael Slawinski, December 1999.

95 Mossy's 5.10 WI5, 35 m, FA: Andrew Shephard, Brandon Thomas, December 1996.

20 Mr. Hanky II M6, 30 m, FA: Wiktor Skupinski, Raphael Slawinski, December 1998.

97 Naked Gun M6 WI5, 25 m, FA: Eric Hoogstraten, Greg Thaczuk, Eamonn Walsh, March 1999.

87 Nasty Infection M6, 25 m, FA: Sean Isaac, Graham MacLean, Chuck Sutton, February 2000.

69 Nightmare on Wolf Street V M7+ WI6+, 175 m, FA: Kefira Allen, Sean Isaac, Dave Thomson,
February 1999.

119 Nine Inch Nails M8+ WI5 X, 30 m, FA: Will Gadd, Raphael Slawinski, December 1999.

93 Old Milwaukee III M7, 50 m, FA: Bill Belcourt, Steve House, December 1996.

123 Oo La La M8, 50 m, FA: Dave Thomson, March 2000.

120 Opaque Idiots 5.8 WI4 (M5), 50 m, FA: Sean Isaac, Dave Thomson, March 1996.

43 Overhang, The M6, 15 m, FA: unknown, winter 1998/1999.

43 Pascquala M6, 20 m, FA: Sean Isaac, March 1998.

131 Pee Bottle Matters M4, 30 m, FA: Cory Balano, Dave Edgar, Dave Marra, March 2000.

20 Pipimenchen 5.6 A1 WI4, 90 m, FA: Jeff Everett, Bob Lee, Glen Reisenhofer, November 1992.

31 Pity us Fools IV 5.7 WI5+, 70 m, FA: Graham Maclean, Rob Owens, November 1999.

30 Plastic Exploding Universe M7 WI5, 60 m, FRA: Jack Roberts, Miles Smart, November 1999.

117 Power to Burn M9, 25 m, FA: Will Gadd, December 1999.

138 Pure Joy M5, 25 m, FA: Eric Hoogstraten, Eamonn Walsh, March 2000.

87 Put on Your Huggies M5+, 20 m, FA: Guy Lacelle, Dave Thomson, December 1999.

95 Quivering Buttcheeks III 5.9 M5 WI5, 30 m, FA: Barry Blanchard, Jack Tackle,
   January 1997. FFA: Allan Massin, Geoff Trump, January 1997.

45 Razor Blade IV M5 WI4 R, 125 m, FA: Allan Massin, Cory Ogle, November 1996.

33 Real Big Drip, The V M7+ WI7, 200 m, FA: Kafira Allen, Eric Dumerac, Sean Isaac,
   Dave Thomson, December 1998.

25 Red Man Soars III 5.10- WI4+ (M5+), 55 m, FA: Barry Blanchard, Joe Josephson, Tim
   Pochay, December 1993. FFA: Doug Heinrich, Alex Lowe, December 1994.
   Direct Start: Bruce Hendricks, Paul Valuilis, November 1995.

23 Ribbon of Darkness III 5.7 WI5, 50 m, FA: Dave Campbell, Jeff Everett,
   Glen Reisenhofer, December 1994.

87 River Runs Through It, The M6, 25 m, FA: Guy Lacelle, Dave Thomson, December 1999.

57 Rock On and Off II 5.8 WI3, 50 m, FA: Allan Massin, Steve Pratt, December 1993.

113 Rocket Man VI M7+ WI5+, 350 m, FA: Kafira Allen, Eric Dumerac, Raphael Slawinski,
   Dave Thomson, April 1999.

109 Route With No Name V WI5+ R, 350 m, FA: Keith Haberl, Richard Jagger, Ryan Johnstone,
   Brian Spear, November 1993.

52 Sea of Vapors V 5.8 WI5+ (M5), 165 m, FA: Bruce Hendricks, Joe Josephson
   February 1993.

42 Secret Samadhi M5+, 12 m, FA: Hermien Freriksen, Shawn Huisman, Sean Isaac, March 1999.

83 Shagadelic M7, 15 m, FA: Jim Gudjonson, Sean Isaac, February 2000.

55 Shampoo Planet III 5.9 WI3 R (M5), 190 m, FA: Peter Arbic, Joe Buszowski, November 1992.

95 Shooter Bar M7, 30 m, FA: Jim Gudjonson, Abby Watkins, March 2000.

97 Silent Sam M7, 30 m, FA: Jim Gudjonson, January 2000.

79 Sinus Gully IV 5.6 WI3, 75 m, FA: Bugs McKeith, John Lauchlan, February 1974.

42 Sketch and Sniff M6+, 12 m, FA: Eamonn Walsh, Scott Withers, November 1998.

129 Slaughterhouse M8+, 30 m, FA: Sean Isaac, Chuck Sutton, February 2000.

37 Snowbird M6+, 40 m, FA: Shawn Huisman, March 2000.

139 Spanish Fly WI4+ 5.9, 30 m, FA: Sean Elliott, Martin Garcia, January 2000.

 87 Splashdown M5, 25 m, FA: Guy Lacelle, Dave Thomson, December 1999.

124 Stairway to Heaven IV M7+ WI5, 95 m, FA: Kefira Allen, Eric Dumerac, Dave Thomson, April 1998.

 52 Stuck in the Middle V M7 WI6, 145 m, FA: Patricia Deavoll, Rob Owens, February 2000.

 76 Suffer Machine V 5.6 A1 WI5, 200 m, FA: Jeff Everett, Glen Reisenhofer, April 1991.

 61 Superlight V 5.10 M6 WI5+, 230 m, FA: Will Gadd, Laurence Monnyeur, Bruno Sourzac, March 1999.

 87 Surfin' Safari M5, 25 m, FA: Guy Lacelle, Dave Thomson, December 1999.

 53 Svoboda M9, 25 m, FA: Greg Thaczuk, Jyoti Venne, April 2000.

 83 Swank M8-,15 m, FA: Sean Isaac, December 1999.

 88 Swine Dive M7, 30 m, FA: Dave Thomson, March 1997.

 52 T2 V 5.9 A0 WI6+, 150 m, FA: Serge Angelucci, Jeff Everett, January 1993.

 76 Teddy Bear's Picnic V M8 WI6, 200 m, FA: Sean Isaac, Dave Thomson, October 1997.

 64 Teenage Yachty IV M5+, 70 m, FA: Sean Isaac, Dave Thomson, Tom Wolfe, March 1997.

 45 Ten Years After IV 5.9 WI5+, 145 m, FA: Keith Haberl, Ken Wylie, October 1996.
     Direct Start: Dave Thomson, Tom Wolfe, October 1996.

 30 Thin Universe M7 WI4 R, 40 m, FA: Dion Bretzloff, Eric Dumerac, November 1997.

117 This is the End Ever M5+ R, 30 m, FA: Ben Firth, Greg Thaczuk, Jyoti Venne,
     Eamonn Walsh, December 1999.

 88 Throttler M7-, 30 m, FA: Dave Thomson, February 1997.

 44 Trans-Canada Iceway IV M5 WI4 R, 180 m, FA: Serge Angelucci, Allan Massin, November 1992.

 52 Troubled Dreams V M7 WI6, 145 m, FA: Scott Backes, Bruce Hendricks, March 1996.
     FFA: Alex Lowe, Dave Bangert, March 1996.

 92 Twisted III 5.9 WI3 R, 120 m, FA: Paul Obanhein, Craig Reason, January 1985.

 40 Twisted Sister IV 5.7 R WI4, 300 m, FA: Frank Campbell, Karl Nagy, J. A. Owen,
     November 1988.

 46 Two Piece Yanks V 5.11 WI7 (M6+), 225 m, FA: Steve House, Stan Price, March 1997.

 43 Tyranny of Gear, The M7, 20 m, FA: Steve House, Joe Josephson, Mark Price, March 1998.

113 U2 III M7+ WI5+ R, 60 m, FA: Ben Firth, Rob Owens, Raphael Slawinski,
     Eamonn Walsh, January 2000.

137 Unicorn IV M7-, 80 m, FA: Eric Dumerac, Dave Thomson, March 1998.

 72 Uniform Queen V 5.8 M7- WI5, 170 m, FA: Sean Isaac, Dave Thomson, November 1997.

 99 Up a Tree M? WI4+, 70 m, FA: Steve Pratt, Allan Massin, February 1998.

 95 Wart Hog M5 WI6, 45 m, FA: Dave Chase, Grant Statham, Brad Wrobleski, March 1995.

 25 White Man Soars III 5.9+ R WI6, 55 m, FA: Steve House, Stan Price, March 1997.

 98 White Ribbon, The III 5.8 R WI4, 280 m, FA: Klas Shock, Geoff Trump, February 2000.

111 With or Without You III M6+ WI4+, 65 m, FA: Rob Owens, Raphael Slawinski,
     Eamonn Walsh, January 2000.

 98 WWF III M6 WI4+, 100 m, FRA: Allan Massin, Steve Pratt, February 1998.
     FFA: Rob Owens, Eamonn Walsh, November 1999.